· THE ·
Parenting Plan Handbook

A Four-Part Video Guide to Skillfully Building a Strong, Child-Centered Parenting Plan

Karen Bonnell, ARNP, MS,

Divorce / Co-Parenting Coach with

Felicia Malsby Soleil, JD, Attorney / Mediator

A NOTE TO THE VIEWER/READER:

This material, including the videos and this workbook, are designed to provide information about the subject matters covered. It is sold with the understanding that neither the authors, nor any contributors, are giving legal, mental health, or other professional advice or services within the material. If expert assistance, legal services or counseling is needed, the viewer/reader should find and use the services of licensed professionals in their jurisdiction. The authors assume no responsibility for any damages incurred during or as a result of using this information.

The names of certain individuals were changed to protect their privacy.

The Parenting Plan Handbook: A Four-Part Video Guide for Skillfully Building a Strong, Child-Centered Parenting Plan

ISBN-13: 978-1516917419
ISBN-10: 1516917413
LCCN: 2015915498

Printed in the United States of America by CreateSpace.
Published in the United States of America by
CMC Publishers, Bellevue, Washington.
www.theparentingplanhandbook.com
www.coachmediateconsult.com

~~~~~~~~~~~~~~~~~~~~~~~~~~~~~~~~~

DEDICATION

We dedicate this video guide and workbook to our clients, colleagues,
and to the Collaborative Law and mediation communities.

To putting "family" back in the center of family law.

We offer this video guide and workbook to parents
everywhere as they skillfully restructure their families.

To keeping kids central and co-parents supported.

~~~~~~~~~~~~~~~~~~~~~~~~~~~~~~~~~

Insight & Inspiration:

All That We Learn in the Process is What Matters Most...

Looking back is quite a journey.... As an almost 60 year old woman looking back at what the 23-25 year old was dealing with, I feel such compassion. Sometimes I wonder, "How the hell do we all get through the pain in our lives?" Then I realize it is through our connection with others, with spirit, and with ourselves, that we grow through it all. I am grateful that life has become peaceful and full of joy. We sometimes can't predict the tough times or prevent them from happening. Who we are as we go through those times, and all we learn in the process, is what matters most.

—**Margy Clair**, MC, LMHC is a life coach and author of *The 5 Steps to Forgiveness* practicing in Gig Harbor, Washington: **www.covisionwellness.com**

CONTENTS

VIDEO I

VIDEO II

VIDEO III

VIDEO IV

VIDEO I CONTENT OUTLINES

YOU NEED A PARENTING PLAN
Facing Divorce/Separation

Chapter 1: Creating a Parenting Plan

- Appreciating that divorce is a family matter with legal implications
- Recognizing that divorce doesn't delete a family for kids
- Facing divorce as a "D" word—will my children be disadvantaged?
- Building a foundation for the future—transparency, integrity and trust
- Doubting your decision may lead to discernment when considering divorce
- Grasping what makes divorce destructive for kids
- Shielding your children from adult hostile conflict
- Putting kids in the middle or losing contact with a parent hurts
- Remembering kids don't cause divorce and they can't solve adult problems
- Pursuing a 'good divorce' for kids
- Being your children's *confident guide* as you restructure the family
- Considering when to tell your children about the divorce / separation
- Recognizing that in the absence of good information, children will make things up
- Introducing the New Model—keeping kids and family central and out of court
- Incorporating the "C" words of a good divorce into your divorce process

Chapter 2: Keeping Kids Central

- Stepping out of blame and judgment—working toward a positive future
- Knowing what's best for kids is two "good enough" parents both engaged!
- Visualizing: Your child's high school graduation
- Recognizing strong co-parenting prevents kids from "guessing or stressing"
- Uncoupling—the opposite of love is indifference
- Understanding the financial and emotional impact of unnecessary conflict on your legal process
- Grieving as an important part of divorce / separation
- Facing serious challenges: high conflict and other complex adult issues
- Considering special needs for one or more of your children
- Building a parenting plan for an unborn child and infants

Chapter 3: Building Your Team

- Choosing a legal process for divorce / separation—considering the options
- Choosing highly trained divorce professionals who are available to help you succeed
- Stepping back from advice that raises conflict—trusting a collaborative approach
- Choosing the right family and child-centered lawyer for you
- Recapping your emotional preparation and elements of the New Model

Chapter 4: Creating Your Co-Parenting Goals

- Crafting your co-parenting goals
- Offering practical advice as you enter your co-parenting process
- Transforming "fighting for my kids" into "we're fighting for *our* kids"
- Encouraging respectful communication and healthy boundaries
- Making joint decisions before changing our financial arrangement
- Following the rule of thumb: parents first—dating second
- Considering when to seek legal advice

Chapter 5: Creating a Temporary Duty-Parent Schedule

- Beginning to co-parent while you continue to reside in the same home
- Defining duty parent and guest parent
- Maintaining children's rhythms while maximizing parent time in tandem
- Sharing parenting responsibilities and building new skills
- Defining your new duties and roles as a co-parent
- Practicing your new roles and building trust as co-parents in the same house
- Rotating in and out of the house to care for children—"Bird-Nesting"
- Utilizing a facilitator may help co-parents sort out the details and get off on the right foot
- Considering guidelines for co-parent planning meetings

VIDEO II CONTENT OUTLINES

DESIGNING YOUR RESIDENTIAL SCHEDULE
Sharing Your Children Across Two Homes

Chapter 6: Designing Your Residential Schedule—Developmental Considerations

- Dealing with the grief that comes with the loss of time and contact with your children
- Wrestling and letting go of feelings of possessiveness and competition
- Updating your language: custody and visitation become parenting time and residential parent
- Building new rhythms for a new normal in your children's changing family
- Growing the residential schedules, building in tiers—developmental steps
- Preparing children for a residential schedule
- Practicing a schedule builds confidence and competence
- Keeping siblings on the same rhythm
- Crafting a schedule for young children
- Considering the needs of teens and young adults
- Following the daily residential schedule —"The River" holds the rhythm / pattern underneath the flow of life
- Turning the parents' struggle over the schedule into learning about kids with professional help
- Reviewing: what's good for kids when families restructure

Chapter 7: Residential Schedules for School-age Children

- Understanding the proper legal forms in your jurisdiction
- Remembering *what's important* in creating schedules that support kids
- Defining a "shared parenting schedule" as enough time for a sense of home with each parent
- Building successful shared schedules
- Providing children what they need defines being a "good parent"
- Understanding when a "primary parenting schedule" may be appropriate
- Solving scheduling issues while remaining two 100% parents
- Avoiding the pitfall of counting hours / counting days
- Examining the pros and cons of Right of First Refusal
- Re-building trust through respect and predictability is related to flexibility long term

Chapter 8: Summer Schedules and Vacations with Parents

- Defining summer break and looking for opportunities to extend time for a parent
- Adjusting the residential schedule to fit the activities and intent of summer vacation
- Using summer break to initiate changes to the school schedule prior to school resuming allows kids to adjust more easily
- Planning summer vacation with parents

- Vacationing and developmental appropriate considerations for children
- Underlying practical considerations: flexibility, cooperation, communicating

Chapter 9: Scheduling School Breaks

- Defining the school breaks
- Considering parents' work schedules
- Planning for and prioritizing travel options
- Handling child care during breaks

Chapter 10: Scheduling Holidays and Celebrations

- Giving consideration to rituals, traditions, and extended family gatherings
- Preserving some traditions and creating new traditions in the short-term
- Allowing for long-term adjustment that reflects family growth
- Planning rotations and sharing between parents, extended family and friends
- Matching holidays with school break schedules
- Swapping weekends—an option to create balance
- Defining single holidays that adjoin with weekends
- Determining importance of holidays that fall during the summer break
- Understanding options: holidays on a holiday schedule or regular daily schedule
- Dividing and conquering, sharing, or celebrating in tandem—holiday options

Chapter 11: Scheduling Special Occasions

- Celebrating Mother's Day/Father's Day
- Helping your children prepare to celebrate the important people they love
- Thinking about birthdays—yours and your children's—options and considerations
- Celebrating birthdays together
- Planning children's birthdays: both family-based parties and with peers
- Identifying a project manager for children's peer birthday parties
- Reviewing the various "business roles" for co-parents
- Considering birthday party budgets
- Welcoming each other—and when the time comes, welcoming domestic partners
- Identifying other events and occasions unique to you and your family
- Mapping a two to three year schedule on a calendar for clarity

VIDEO III CONTENT OUTLINES

TRANSITIONS, COMMUNICATION & DECISION-MAKING
Other Important Factors in Your Parenting Plan

Chapter 12: Child-Centered Transitions—Smoothing the Wrinkles in Two-Home Family Life

- Striving for a concise and complete parenting plan
- Understanding the emotional impact of transitions on kids
- Identifying other transition location options
- Co-parenting agreements for easing transitions
- Transitioning children's belongings

Chapter 13: Communication Protocols—Sharing Information and Staying Connected

- Agreeing on a communication plan
- Writing transition reports
- Keeping each other informed about extraordinary child-related information
- Navigating differences in parenting
- Agreeing on methods of communicating
- Using Billy Eddy's BIFF: Brief, Informative, Firm, & Friendly
- Communicating with the children when they're not in residence
- Communicating when the kids are traveling
- Communicating with professionals

Chapter 14: Decision Making—Parents as Co-Parent Executive Officers

- Appreciating the types of medical decisions
- Separating facts from values simplifies decision making
- Understanding education decisions
- Examining religious decisions
- Exploring other options for joint decision-making
- Sharing a list of child-care providers
- Examining Right of First Refusal and how that provision relates to other child-care options
- Utilizing your co-parent meetings for schedule planning and decision making
- Getting the help you need to be successful

Chapter 15: Paying for Children's Needs and Activities—Extraordinary Expenses, Kids and Money

- Understanding how decision making and child support intertwine
- Protecting your children from conflict over money
- Teaching children about money
- Identifying values and money management

*Each day of our lives we make deposits
into the memory banks of our children.*

—Charles R. Swindoll

VIDEO IV CONTENT OUTLINES

CHANGES, CONFLICT RESOLUTION & CO-PARENTING:
Additional Guidelines for Completing Your Parenting Plan

Chapter 16: Change—Short term, Expected and Unexpected, and Significant Long term Change

- Recognizing the impact of change and causes of conflict
- Trading and swapping time
- Pursuing stability first—flexibility second
- Taking responsibility for business travel and the impact on the residential schedule
- Adjusting the residential schedule—determining the importance of holidays that fall during the summer break
- Ensuring a plan for emergencies and other special considerations
- Managing unusual work schedules
- Implementing expected changes to the schedule based on developmental steps
- Dealing with long-term changes: significant work schedule changes, relocation with or without children
- Renegotiating the residential schedule—crafting new agreements
- Checking with your legal counsel

Chapter 17: Conflict Resolution—Setting Priorities, Solving Problems

- Handling conflict related to competing priorities or overlaps in schedules
- Ranking what's important in terms of "priorities"
- Valuing the children's experience or a parent's need?
- Utilizing the conflict resolution process
- Implementing the steps of a conflict resolution process
- Going to court—the last resort
- Taking steps to resolve conflict with your co-parent

Chapter 18: Co-Parenting Guidelines—Successful Co-Parenting for Your Children's Future

- Co-parenting guidelines
- Establishing the hallmarks of strong co-parenting
- Integrating family life for kids, discipline, and differences in parenting style
- Striving for two "good enough" parents for healthy kids
- Coaching and other resources to help you succeed as co-parents
- Adding new tools to your toolbox
- Using established safety guidelines to help manage conflict
- Ensuring safety when there is a gun in the home with children
- Coming to compromise when belief systems conflict
- Introducing new romantic partners and defining their role
- Blending families—step-parent planning
- Remaining the Co-parent Executive Officers for your children

Chapter 19: Co-Parenting Alone—What if Your Co-Parent Won't Co-Parent?

- Following and modeling guidelines even when your co-parent isn't ready or won't participate
- Setting the bar—have faith in the potential of a better future
- Defining and becoming "who you are"—your best self
- Recapping and appreciating

FOREWORD

Books that are dedicated to the art of parenting are books written for those who answer to a higher calling. A book for parents is a book for innovators, inventors, alchemists, explorers, adventurers, and doers. And when we partake in the making of such a book, or add to its value in any way, we are partaking in a deed truly honorable. I myself am an author of a parenting book, and I'm happy to add to the value of any other good tools for parents that are out there.

I first became acquainted with Karen Bonnell when she asked if she might quote my writing in her previous work, *The Co-Parents' Handbook*. I was happy to share my words with her then, and I am delighted to receive an invitation to now contribute to her latest creation, *The Parenting Plan Handbook*.

I believe in fostering friendly and kindhearted blended and expanded families. I believe the essence of "family" can extend beyond the confines of a marriage contract and beyond the limits of what we expect a family unit to look like. When a marriage or an intimate partnership ends, should the concept and the essence of kindheartedness and goodwill dissolve along with the disintegration of an initial promise? I don't think so! I believe that the essence, the fragrance of the bonds that tie parent and child together, are spiritual connections that go far beyond the limits of paperwork and promises. New promises can always be made when old ones can no longer be kept. Moreover, when we make new promises to new people, we need to do so knowing that their children, whom they love, will become our own children, whom we will love as well.

We've vowed so much more when we have our own kids. Once we've entered this realm, our commitment as parents to the physical, emotional, and mental well-being of our children remains a central and core aspect of family life in whatever forms "family" might take, now and in the future. To our children, both parents become *their family*, and whomever their parents choose to love in the future becomes *their family*, as well.

It is because I believe these things that I believe in Karen's co-parenting philosophy, and I now look forward to her newest handbook, *The Parenting Plan Handbook*. Karen Bonnell, and her co-author Felicia Malsby Soleil, are peacekeepers at heart. Their hopeful contribution to ushering in peace for families in transition is a work of daily dedication as they guide others toward resolving conflicts that can otherwise be so destructive to their co-parenting relationships, and for the well-being of all the children that are involved. I am grateful to be part of this endeavor, and I am happy to meet all of you here in this foreword and to join you on the journey of discovering what Karen and Felicia have in store for us all, this time around!

—C. JoyBell C.

An author of philosophy of mind, poetry, fiction,

and other things wise and wonderful.

INTRODUCTION

When my son was little, my favorite part of the day was bath time. My son's three year-old-body would start wiggling at the dinner table in anticipation of the fun that lay ahead. He would race to the bathroom, carefully review his bins of bath toys, and chuck everything into the tub. He would "help" pour the bubble bath and delight in the mountains of bubbles that resulted. There were shark attacks and splashes, songs and the preschool equivalent of knock-knock jokes. As a working mother, I loved this time together. It felt like the one part of the day when I could be fully present, enjoying this funny kid, undistracted by the stresses and strains of life outside the bathtub.

One night, we were singing some of our old standards when he started switching up the words. Instead of "Mommy's taking me to the zoo tomorrow," he sang, "Mommy AND Daddy taking me to the zoo tomorrow." His dad and I had been divorced for about a year, and my response to the change in lyrics must have been lukewarm because my son suddenly shot to his feet (in the slippery tub!), put his hands on his hips and tearfully shouted, "You no liking my daddy!"

I was stunned. To make matters worse, he went on to name my parents and a close girlfriend as also "no liking" his daddy. I still can't quite recall how I got him to sit down or what I even said in response to his bubble-covered accusation. What I do know is that my heart broke.

If you're reading this, you already know what I (sadly) had to be reminded of: children want to love and be loved by BOTH parents. This is a child's birthright, a guarantee that should be put in writing alongside length and weight on the birth certificate: "Your parents will love you to death, and you can love them back all you want, *no matter what*."

But again, I know that you know this. I know this because you are smartly and sensitively reading this book and following the incomparable advice being offered to you by its authors.

Karen Bonnell and Felicia Malsby Soleil have devoted their entire professional lives to families experiencing the (sometimes) indescribable pain of divorce. They have spent hours advising, coaching, observing and listening and, lucky for us all, they have turned those hours into the incredible resource you have at your disposal. This book and the accompanying video series offer a level of competent, compassionate co-parenting assistance that every divorcing family should experience. If you do the work and follow their warm, professional guidance, you and your child (or children) will emerge from the divorce healthy, intact, and with a strong foundation for the post-divorce life that is ahead.

My son is now a lanky 21 year-old with a sweet smile and a deep love of chemistry. He has step-parents, half-siblings, step-siblings, grandparents, aunties, uncles, and cousins galore. He loves them all and has benefited so much from his relationships with them. After that fateful bath so many years ago, I tucked my son into bed and called his dad. We each took a deep breath and did what needed to be done. So will you.

—**Jamie Kautz**, MSN, LICSW

Child and family therapist

HOW TO USE
"THE PARENTING PLAN HANDBOOK"
WORKBOOK

Welcome to your companion workbook—specifically designed to complement and enhance the four-part video guide portion of "The Parenting Plan Handbook." We invite you to utilize your workbook in tandem with watching each video. **Information for streaming the videos can be found by going to www.theparentingplanhandbook.com.** You will find the following assets included:

- **Insights & Inspirations**—a chorus of voices from professionals and parents around the world to support you in your process.

- **Lighthouses**—important information that emphasizes how to stay child-centered while building a skillful parenting plan.

- **Journal Pages**—thought provoking questions that deepen your thought process and prepare you for the final step.

- **Parenting Plan Worksheets**—a comprehensive set of worksheets that once completed provide a solid foundation for constructing a strong, child-centered parenting plan.

We're so glad you're here. We look forward to walking with you through the videos and hope you feel our support as you explore your workbook and complete your parenting plan worksheets. We acknowledge the influence of practicing in our region, our state, and our country on our language and understanding of parenting plan elements. Children are children everywhere—how you plan to care for them as you restructure your family has many shared elements, and how you document those for a parenting plan will be specific to your jurisdiction. We trust you'll translate as needed the concepts and principles to fit your particular jurisdiction and, more importantly, your family's needs.

—**Karen** & **Felicia**

IMPORTANT
A Parenting Plan is a Legal Document—
Seeking Legal Counsel is Strongly Encouraged

In developing this material, the authors recognize that they cannot address the legal implications unique to each specific jurisdiction in which their readers reside. Their goal is to present comprehensive information and practical advice (NOT legal or therapeutic advice) that applies to developing your role as successful co-parents, regardless of your geographic location.

The parenting plan worksheets contained in this workbook are designed to help you discuss and craft with your co-parent the language and terms you would like to ultimately see in your final legal document, (commonly known as a Parenting Plan).

You are strongly encouraged by the authors to seek the advice of legal counsel in your area to assist you with converting your worksheets into the required legal document specific to your jurisdiction, as well as to discuss with you the legal implications of the agreements reached by you and your co-parent.

VIDEO I
YOU NEED A PARENTING PLAN
Facing Divorce / Separation

Insight & Inspiration:

Creating Family Ever After...

In 2004, we chose to retire our marriage after 18 years and embark upon our journey toward a "new normal"—living between "Mommy's House" and "Daddy's House". We sat down as a *family ever after* and laid out what we would include in our roadmap to success. As parents of three young children: six, nine, and 12 years, we made a conscious decision to focus our attention on making this lifestyle as functional and heart-centered as possible.

Our role was crystal-clear: to co-parent our children with the same love, devotion and mindfulness we would have observed under one roof. Was it possible? Of course it was. The same disciplinary rules applied at each household, and if one of the children faced a particular challenge, both parents were part of the solution. All responsibilities were shared equally. As a collaboratively divorced family, we attended every parent-teacher meeting together, believing it showed the children (and the school) they are loved and supported in all ways, planting healthy seeds for successful mindsets.

The manner in which we handled this critical time in their lives would provide our children with essential life skills and tools for the future. As parents we are always teaching, after all. Modeling behaviors we wanted duplicated for the legacy of our children and the next generation was our goal and we do believe that putting our children first in this way over these last 11 years, has proven to have been worth its weight in gold.

—**Carolyn Flower**, owner of Carolyn Flower Enterprises and author of
Gravitate 2 Gratitude—Journey Your Journey resides in Quebec, Canada:
www.carolynflower.com

CHAPTER 1

Creating a Parenting Plan

Insight & Inspiration:

Your Promise to Your Children...

Even if difficult, children adjust to the changes that come with divorce. What children cannot sustain is the loss of parents' love and attention, or the loss of their once-in-a-lifetime childhood. Your parenting plan is your promise to your children for a peaceful future. Fulfill that promise.

—**Kristin Little**, MA, MS, LMHC is the contributing author of "The Co-Parents' Handbook", counselor and a Collaborative Law child specialist in the greater Seattle area: **www.kristinlittlecounseling.com**.

When Do You Need a Parenting Plan?

You will need a parenting plan when the nature of your intimate partnership changes through separation or divorce and your children will no longer be residing in only one household. You will also need a parenting plan if you have never lived together and do not intend to live together in one home while parenting and you want to establish a parenting plan as part of a paternity action. In most jurisdictions, this is a required document for completing a legal divorce.

What Does a Parenting Plan Do?

The purpose of a parenting plan is to determine a somewhat predictable and consistent residential schedule for your children between two homes. It can include structure for ages of children from birth through preschool years, during their regular school schedule, summer and other school breaks, and holidays and special occasions. In addition, it establishes protocols for decision making and conflict resolution, as well as addresses a myriad of other provisions unique to you and your family. A well drafted and thoughtful parenting plan can take the guess work out of navigating your new terrain of co-parenting in two households.

Think of the parenting plan as the structure, agreements, and commitments that will enable you to maintain civility and stability for your children's two-home family life. We often say that a parenting plan is the 'default', the conflict manager, the document you return to when you cannot agree and need structure and guidelines to keep the peace while life moves forward.

Protecting Children from a "Bad Divorce"

(The "D" Words: Disadvantaged, Deceit, Destructive, Damage, Destroyed, Doubt...)

We are here to support you through the workbook to do whatever you can to protect your children from the elements that make divorce destructive for kids:

- **Hostile conflict:** Conflict is a part of every relationship, and certainly, every divorce. Working through problems, resolving conflicts big and small, and keeping adult conflict at the adult level gives kids the confidence that you're dealing with the adult stuff and they can be kids free from worry. **Hostile conflict refers to the enmity between two adults that is intended to punish, harm, or create division in the family—forcing children to choose sides to escape the irreconcilable stories, blame, and judgment expressed by their parents.** Reach out for help if you find that you are struggling with high emotions, involving your children, or lapsing into hurtful co-parent bashing.

- **Children caught in the middle:** There are many ways that children (young and old) can feel caught in the middle: **keeping secrets for a parent, delivering hostile information from one parent to the other, hearing the conflict over their parents' divorce and feeling forced to pick sides, interrogating a child to get information about the other parent's life (asking your child to be a private eye!).** These experiences are distressing and harmful to kids.

- **Emotional overwhelm:** Self-care is essential. You are in the middle of a huge family change, life change—everything may be shifting. Call in your supports! Your children need you to stay enough in-the-saddle of family life that they can remain safely and securely in their childhood. **Asking children to have the emotional maturity to take care of adults, take over responsibility for the household or younger siblings before they have the skill or maturity to handle the pressure, is hard on kids—and in some cases, not safe.** Take good care of yourself so you can take good care of your kids.

- **Loss of relationship with a parent:** Children benefit from a strong and engaged relationship with two "good enough" parents. **In the face of so much loss and pain, a parent might be tempted to use the children as a weapon against a co-parent—as punishment for leaving the marriage or as leverage in property settlement. Or equally concerning, is when a parent devolves into competing for the children** and using phrases like, "it's in the best interest of the kids to be *with me*—I'm the better parent." This may represent stability, or a version of the past, or may be the cost you feel your co-parent should pay for leaving the marriage. Think through how to support your children's love for both of you; consider their health by supporting an engaged relationship with each of you. If you are entering a new romantic relationship, remember: parent first, date second. Your children need *just you* right now, and will grow to be ready for new adults in their life after a sufficient period of stability and security.

Divorce does not have to be destructive. Be aware of the potholes: toxic conflict, getting caught in the middle and having to choose sides against a parent, or losing a parent from emotional overwhelm, lack of access, or through a new relationship that disrupts the opportunity to stabilize. Skillfully transitioning your children's sense of family is an enormous gift to them today and for their entire future.

Half of your child's heart belongs to each of you.
Your conflict becomes the conflict in their hearts.

Separating Spouse Mind from Parent Mind

One of the toughest challenges early in a separation / divorce process is sorting through the myriad of feelings triggered by ending your intimate partnership and facing the changes precipitated by that decision. You are forced to do all this emotional work while holding your ground *as a parent*.

Most parents find their judgment clouded, and experience feeling distracted, easily frustrated, and sometimes just plain emotionally exhausted. The kids are going through their own feelings and responding to the stress in the household. You want to show up and parent effectively. And, for your kids' sake, you're hoping your co-parent will show up effectively, too. Even though you may be hurt or mad, do your best not to throw gasoline on the emotional fire.

The upset thoughts and feelings about ending your intimate partnership come from your spouse mind. Like a talk-radio station, you may hear a steady monologue of rants and protests, criticisms and blame. All part of working through grief and acceptance, all in the service of processing the anger and hurt over loss.

There is a healthy amount of processing emotions. However, this adult-relationship upset is not healthy to share with kids. This is *your* work. The upset about your intimate partner is part of your spouse mind, and reflects issues between adults. Kids don't create adult problems and kids can't solve them. Don't involve them—they are helpless to do anything constructive with your feelings. Involving them as allies may provide temporary relief for you, but is destructive for them.

Your parent-mind radio station broadcasts reminders that your children love both of you, need both of you, and benefit from having a close parental relationship with each of you. You are instructed to protect their hearts from adult conflict and negative comments about their other parent. Your parent-mind voice reminds you to support them in loving each of you openly without fear of hurting anyone. You are prompted to share information with your co-parent that will help him / her be successful as a parent. Keep your parent-mind radio station tuned in as best you can. That's best for kids.

Qualities of a Good Divorce...
What's BEST for Kids!

A good way to remember what's best for kids—the **C**-Words. You and your co-parent can hold these skills as lighthouses of your divorce.

- **Cordial Communication:** Be sure that all forms of **c**ommunication are **c**olleague-style, respectful, **c**ivil / **c**ourteous.

- **Cooperation:** Remember that you are BOTH still parents to your amazing kids—keep the kids **c**entral without allowing them to get caught in the middle.

- **Collaboration:** Solve problems together—**c**reate a strong two-home family life, respecting each other, maintaining respectful boundaries, and **c**aring for your **c**hildren without interfering with the other parent.

- **Conflict Managed:** Keep **c**onflict resolution front of mind, **c**onstructive and problem-solving oriented.

- **Co-Parenting:** Be **c**onfident guides, with both of you engaged, **c**aring and learning how to tandem parent—rebuilding a secure base across both homes.

There are a few other **child-centered** considerations we want to emphasize:

- **Caring Communication:** In discussing your children's other parent and / or family, take **c**are of your children's heart.

- **Loving Freely:** Your children will thrive when they can love each of you freely and express that openly.

- **Predictability and Secure Base:** Children thrive when things are reasonably predictable (like their schedule with each parent and to some extent their daily rhythms) and their relationship with each of you is secure. Recognize the power of strong co-parenting for your child's physical and emotional health.

- **Children's Belongings:** Remember their belongings belong to them. Allow kids to move their special items, their clothes, their gear back and forth, without fear or concern or pressure.

- **Sense of Home with each Parent:** Although a child has two residences, their *sense of home* and family can be inclusive of both. Create a sense of home that extends across residences for your children.

"For a child's sense of family, what divorce breaks apart,
strong co-parenting rebuilds."

When Should We Tell the Kids?

When and what to tell your children about the decision to become a two-home family has much to do with their ages. Younger children (under age 8) do better with less than seven to ten days lead time between telling them something is going to change and the beginning of the change. The change doesn't have to be abrupt, so the more you think through and carefully pace the transition, the smoother it will be for the kids.

Older children can understand that you've made a decision and it will take a bit longer to implement. Older children benefit from watching you work together as parents for as long as a month or more prior to one of you actually moving out or making a similar change in the structure of the family. The important issue here is that they are clear that you have made a final decision, that you're taking steps forward, and that they have no role in reversing the course of this important family change.

The key is your ability to work together as parents: managing conflict, solving problems, sharing child-care duties in a planned way, while taking steps to transition the family to a new structure.

Remember: you are changing your adult relationship, ending an intimate partnership. Your children aren't a part of that highly personal adult relationship—and have limited ability to understand intimate partnership (even teens). Although your intimate partnership is completing or ending, *parents and children don't divorce.*

You are building a new co-parenting relationship—and yet there is nothing new about being parents to your children. What is new is how you will share them throughout the days, weeks and years ahead and how you integrate their lives across two homes. Your co-parenting relationship directly affects your children and matters most to them. "Who will tuck me in and read stories?" "Who will help me with my homework?" "Who will take me to driver's ed?"

For a brief **video on "How to Tell Your Children About Divorce / Separation,"** please go to **http://coachmediate-consult.com/co-parents-handbook/**

A New Model

Children are the same all over the world. They love their parents. They need to be safe and secure with them, and loved by them to thrive in adult life. Ireland only introduced divorce in 1997 so we have been able to learn from the experiences of other countries. Divorce causes huge emotional upset for children, but we now know continuing conflict over the children causes the most harm. We must hear what children (often as adults) have told us about what it was like for them and what they needed at that time. This is what I've learned:

For parents:

- Listen to your children, what they say and how they feel.
- Hear the voices of other children through books, DVDs and learn.
- Separate the "couple relationship" from your "parenting relationship."
- Strive to put the children first no matter what your "ex" might do.

For lawyers:

- Signpost child support services and non adversarial processes at the outset.
- Be challenging of any bad behavior in clients.
- Develop a good working relationship with the lawyer for the other parent.
- Don't rush to Court.

For the Court:

- Signpost mediation and mediation information sessions before any court application is accepted.
- Tell parents what is expected of them in the Court process.
- Be timely and consistent in your rulings.

Being a parent is not always easy but it is particularly difficult during the separation / divorce process. Children do not need perfect parents, so do not be too hard on yourselves. They need to know that you love them and are doing the best you can do.

—**Muriel Walls** is a solicitor, mediator and Collaborative Law practitioner who is recognized internationally as a lecturer on family law matters; she resides in Dublin, Ireland.
www.wallsandtoumey.ie

Journal Moment 1

1) What will help me to bring my best self forward toward creating a healthy co-parenting relationship?

_____

_____

_____

_____

_____

2) How can I help my co-parent do the same?

_____

_____

_____

_____

_____

3) How can my co-parent help me?

_____

_____

_____

_____

_____

CHAPTER 2

Keeping Kids Central

Insight & Inspiration:

What it Means to be Co-Parent Executive Officers...

Is it health versus happiness? Here's one of the most difficult parts of parenting and of creating a child-centered parenting plan: Our goal as healthy parents is to raise healthy children, not necessarily to ensure their happiness. A healthy child can find his or her *own* happiness!

Unfortunately, guilt and exhaustion and depression, addictions and dependencies, often prompt parents to take the easy way out. They attempt to buy their children's happiness, become permissive to placate bad moods or poor choices in exchange for pleasantry, or allow children control over choices they're not emotionally prepared to make wisely.

Clear limits, boundaries and schedules help our children be healthy even though they sometimes evoke rage and protest. Helping them cope with their strong feelings while maintaining healthy boundaries and limits is one of our most important jobs.

"But what about what my kids want?" Listen. Acknowledge. Reassure them that they are heard and let them know that you and their other parent will work together to make the best decisions that you can.

—**Benjamin D. Garber, Ph.D.**, is a psychologist and author practicing in New Hampshire. Dr. Garber's latest book, "Holding Tight, Letting Go" will be available in the fall of 2015. Learn more at **www.HealthyParent.com**.

Everyone's Grieving

Grief is a healthy and natural response to loss and change. Working with grief will be part of restructuring your family. Everyone will experience grief in their own way in their own time. Grief is not an indication that this is a *bad thing* or that someone should be blamed for causing the grief. As parents, you can't prevent your children from facing change—what you can do is help them face challenges and change with compassion and resilience—building coping strategies, which include understanding and working through their feelings.

Children often speak through actions louder than words. Your young child may be throwing more tantrums, lashing out at a sibling, or clinging to you in a way he / she has outgrown. Your school-age child may have developed an uncharacteristic snottiness; your teen, a new-found streak of rebellion or withdrawal. These may all be signs of grieving—a language that says, "All is not right in my world and I'm not sure what to do; can you help me?"

Talk openly and age-appropriately with your children about the stress of change. Provide opportunities for them to identify their feelings and express them directly without you taking offense, blaming their co-parent or feeling blamed. In a supportive way, remind them that everyone is in this together and everyone will find their way through to the other side. Ask them what would help in the moment, and guide them through their own self-care strategies.

If you are concerned about your children, reach out to a health-care provider, school counselor, or family therapist. Please don't ignore persistent signs that worry you.

A child specialist who works in Collaborative Divorce is an excellent resource for children whose family is facing divorce—a "coach for the kids" can bring your children's voice into your family change process in a constructive and supportive manner.

"In the end, only three things matter:
how much you loved,
how gently you lived,
and how gracefully you let go of things not meant for you."

—Buddha

Prescribe a Healthy Process

Parents want what is best for their children as reflected in their Parenting Plan. But what happens when there has been a broken relationship between a parent and a child?

In complex cases where one parent is impaired with addictions, incarcerated, has been physically or sexually abusive, the parenting plan process may need to include recommendations for reconciliation (also referred to as reunification counseling) between the child and the distressed/estranged parent. Please get wise counsel on the best way to ensure that your children are protected from their parent's impairment while simultaneously understanding the value of a relationship with each parent.

The steps in a reconciliation process should be skillfully and thoroughly considered with appropriate safeguards; no one has a way of guaranteeing an outcome. You can require a process, but you can't require a relationship. Both parents must understand this reality. Otherwise, the children may be the ones caught in the middle—forced to comply with a process that is not effective with a parent who may not be prepared to constructively parent or safely engage in a trust-building relationship.

Use your divorce team to help discern the best steps for a safe and healthy process that create the potential for a positive outcome. This may mean a pause in the relationship between a child and a parent while the parent completes treatment and builds his / her own stability prior to any reconciliation or reunification efforts.

—**Wendi Schuller** is a nurse, and author of *The Global Guide to Divorce* published by
Austin Macauley, London, October, 2015.
www.globalguidetodivorce.com

Journal Moment 2

1. What are my greatest challenges as I consider my parenting planning process?

_____

_____

_____

_____

_____

_____

_____

_____

_____

_____

~~~~~~

"I won't let the mistakes and failures of our marriage
tumble forward and become the mistakes and failures of our co-parenting.
This I commit to you and to our children."

—A Co-Parent's Credo

~~~~~~

Basic Information

Date: _____, 20_____.

Parents:	Mother/Father	Mother/Father
Name		
Telephone		
Email		

Children:

Full Name	Birth Date	M/F	Grade/School
.			

Complex Adult Circumstances

☐ Alcohol, drug, or other substance abuse or concern for relapse if sober

☐ Criminal background (whether or not a conviction) of concern

☐ Violence or threats against an adult or child, pet or property

☐ Restraining orders (or equivalent) for either parent

☐ Inappropriate sexual behavior or other acting out

☐ Neglect or abandonment

☐ Past or present involvement with Child Protective Services

☐ History of frequent, unexpected moves or current plans to relocate out of area

☐ Other significant concerns

Special Needs of One or More of Our Children

☐ Developmental disabilities that require special care, resources, skills

☐ Emotional needs that we need to consider / support as we co-parent

☐ Behavioral considerations that we will need to resource and consider

☐ Physical challenges that we will need to plan for and support

☐ Special academic / school-related needs that will need to be addressed

☐ Complex medical needs, severe allergies, or other health concerns

☐ Other significant concerns (please describe below)

I worry about the following concerns: _____

_____

_____

CHAPTER 3

Building Your Team

Insight & Inspiration:

Professionals Dealing with Divorce Have a Moral Duty to Help...

When a couple separates and self-interest, as opposed to mutual interests, governs their thinking, they each may instinctively expect to be under attack. They may say they feel controlled by the other, but deny being controlling. They are often unaware that their actions and words are perceived by the other in much the same way.

Instinct and fear take over; self-preservation can easily dominate thinking. Molehills of concern become mountains of accusation and enmity. A vicious circle ensues.

Words can heal or words can wound, **hurt people hurt people**. It takes a conscious choice by both partners <u>not</u> to be drawn into destructive conflict in such circumstances.

Children, the silent casualties of conflict, need their parents to be the adults, to put their (the children's) needs first, to give them permission to openly love the other parent whatever hurt may have been caused by one adult to the other. It's tough, but it's necessary.

Professionals dealing with divorce and separation have a moral duty to help which partner of the couple they are advising to gain that perspective as well, to help their clients through the grieving process and not allow anxiety and fear to drive escalating conflict. Work to create solutions that always keep children central—as they will need two engaged, functional parents when all is over.

—**Norman Hartnell,** MCIArb M.A. (Cantab) is a family solicitor, mediator, arbitrator and Collaborative lawyer; he is also the Managing Director of The Family Law Company, UK, **www.thefamilylawco.com**.

Self-Determination—the Ability and Right to Control Your Life

Divorce is a family problem, not a legal problem;
unfortunatelythe traditional legal approach
fails to recognize this.

Divorce is not the end of the family; instead, it is a transition to a different family structure. Divorcing couples, if asked, ideally want the new structure to meet their needs and their children's needs. Additionally, most people want ongoing **self-determination** and control over their lives and their children's lives.

But by its very nature, the traditional legal approach takes control away from the couple and resolves issues in narrow ways that do not benefit their family members. First, lawyers practicing in the traditional legal arena only hear one person's viewpoint. Therefore, as an advocate, the lawyers tend to exacerbate the situation by artificially pitting one family member against the other, causing a delicate and complex situation to spiral out of control. And secondly, the court uses its power to apply laws that are standard and insufficient to meet each family's unique needs.

There are ways for divorcing couples to maintain control and self-determination. Mediation and Collaborative Law both offer divorcing couples alternatives to keep control of their lives. The couple makes decisions and crafts agreements that will work for the unique lives of themselves and their children. This is self-determination, the ability and the right to control your own life. Sure, divorcing couples may not agree on everything in the future, but they are the ones who ultimately consider their lifestyles and values in determining what happens in their future.

—**Debra Synovec**, JD, founder of Whole Mediation & Consulting Services
PC, practices in Seattle, Washington: **www.wholemediation.com.**

Divorce Team Members

Divorce Coach: Your guide through the emotional terrain and practical aspects of divorce. A divorce coach will assist with skill-building, help you maintain your balance, and guide you through the necessary steps in completing your divorce, which may include working with your legal counsel.

Child Specialist: To put it simply, a child specialist helps parents use their parenting skills to protect their children's well-being and sense of security during the divorce. The child specialist gives children a voice during this difficult time; a chance to express *"what's helping and what's hurting"* to a neutral professional without putting them in the middle of parental conflict.

Mediator: Mediation is a confidential way for people to resolve conflict and find solutions to complex problems with the help of a neutral mediator who is trained to help people discuss their differences. The mediator does not decide who is right or wrong or issue a decision. Instead, the mediator employs advanced conflict-resolution skills to help co-parents work out their own solutions to their changing family's structure.

Attorney: Whether you wish to retain the services of an attorney for the entirety of your case, or whether you merely wish to engage an attorney on a consultation basis, understand that a legal professional within your jurisdiction can provide helpful insight into crafting a parenting plan that will be accepted by the court. A parenting plan is a legal document. If you and your co-parent struggle with issues that create unnecessary conflict within the scope of your parenting, you want to be sure to understand how certain terms of a parenting plan may be enforced if court intervention is necessary in the future.

Certified Divorce Financial Analyst: Equipped with all the necessary tools for the divorce process, a CDFA is the financial expert on your team. These tasks can range from helping you prepare budgets, creating a comprehensive financial package that you'll utilize in developing your property settlement agreement, to projecting the financial and tax implications of each divorce settlement option.

Personal Counselor: A highly capable and trained mental health professional with experience and understanding of the unique impact of divorce. He or she should be prepared to assist with grief, high emotion, self-soothing and stress management, and guide you into a future with renewed optimism and strength. Please avoid asking your counselor to collude with you by spending your session blaming, labeling, or strategizing how to fight your co-parent. Ask for help in coping with your situation, strengthening your emotional self-care, and holding on to your best self as a parent and co-parent.

Support System: This includes clergy, family, friends... ask each and every one of your trusted inner circle to support you to work through your negative feelings constructively. Know that well-intentioned, but uninformed direction from your support system can actually derail your forward progress and ultimate positive resolution.

When and How Do You Select a Lawyer?

Your selection of a lawyer should not be taken lightly. You will want an attorney who aligns with your values of being family and child-centered. You will want a professional who is experienced with conflict management, rather than conflict escalation. Most importantly, you will want a legal professional who will be a trustworthy sounding board and can guide you through your family's transition with expert and helpful advice, encouragement, and support.

The best time to consult with an attorney is when you find yourself in a position of making a significant change in your family, typically when you and your intimate partner have decided that your relationship will end. You do not need to wait until you have moved into two separate homes before you seek legal counsel. **In fact, it is encouraged that you seek advice prior to physically separating, if possible, because sometimes you can learn important and creative ways to begin your evolution as co-parents while still under the same roof.**

In the event you do not feel legal counsel is necessary at the beginning of your transition, by all means, you are encouraged to engage an attorney at the time when you need to create a parenting plan for purposes of your separation or divorce or paternity action. Whether you have legal counsel help you construct your parenting plan, explain to you the legal implications of your parenting plan decisions, or simply review your document once you and your co-parent have it drafted, it is always a wise decision to have someone in your jurisdiction look it over for proper form before asking the court to sign off on it.

Journal Moment 3

What Divorce Process Have I Chosen?

☐ We're going to do it ourselves with assistance from team members as needed.

☐ We'll utilize a single mediator to help us with both property / financial and parenting plan aspects.

☐ We're engaging two mediators: one helping us with the property settlement, the other with parenting.

☐ We've opted for co-mediation with a legal or financial professional working with a mental health professional to help us complete our process.

☐ We'll use a single attorney to help us both with legal process, drafting documents, etc. Neither of us will be represented by him/her.

☐ We've determined that a family-centered or Collaborative Law process with two attorneys and suggested team members is best.

☐ Our circumstances suggest that we'd be best accessing a traditional litigation / court-oriented process with two attorneys.

Who Belongs on My Divorce Team?

• Help through the legal process:

    ☐ Attorney

    ☐ Mediator

    ☐ Divorce Coach

    ☐ Other

• Help through the emotional process:

    ☐ Personal counselor

    ☐ Divorce coach

    ☐ Clergy

    ☐ Supportive friends and family

    ☐ Divorce support group

• Help through the property settlement/financial process:

    ☐ Certified divorce financial analyst

    ☐ CPA

    ☐ Financial planner

    ☐ Attorney

• Help with our children and parenting plan:

    ☐ Co-parent / divorce coach

    ☐ Child specialist

    ☐ Child mental health professional

    ☐ Family therapist

    ☐ Children's divorce support group

List your team members and contact information:

_____

_____

_____

_____

CHAPTER 4

Creating Your Co-Parenting Goals

Insight & Inspiration:

The Impact of Our Words...

Two words, "our" and "your," have a direct impact on both the development of the residential schedule and your co-parenting relationship.

Consider the difference between saying "my children" and "our children." How do you feel when you use each term? Think about how your co-parent feels when he / she hears you say "my children" versus "our children". What do you feel when your co-parent says, "my children"?

"Our" is a word of inclusion, of acknowledgment, of invitation.

"My" is a word of exclusion, of separation, of ownership.

Which would you rather experience? What do you want your children to feel?

What seems at first glance to be an easy thing to do is sometimes one of the hardest things to do. Feelings are complicated. We're ending our intimate relationship; we're still parents to "our children".

—**Kevin Scudder, JD** is a Collaborative Law attorney and mediator
in the greater Seattle area: **www.scudderlaw.net**

Building Blocks of a Healthy
Co-Parenting Relationship

☐ Respectful civility

☐ Healthy boundaries

☐ Constructive communication skills

☐ Effective problem-solving skills

☐ Capacity to collaborate, plan, and follow-through

☐ Healthy self-management skills

☐ Emotional maturity

☐ Generosity

☐ Capacity to let go, grieve, and look toward a new future

The Business of Co-Parenting—a Glossary of Terms

Co-Parent Executive Officers: You and your co-parent are the executive team of your children's lives. As you two join forces to confidently guide, lift up, love up and challenge your children to become the adults you know they are capable of becoming, you are tasked with working together toward that end.

- This is a highly skilled relationship that involves respect, boundaries, strong decision making, coordination and communication.
- You are independently making day-to-day decisions in your home, but together, you make decisions about the larger, broader topics / activities / direction of your children's lives.

Co-Parent Financial Officers: You and your co-parent have a financial obligation and relationship predicated on securing the necessary elements of a child's life: basic needs, experiences, resources, health-care, etc. Bringing a business mind to the process and maintaining a strong credit rating with each other allows your children to be free from conflict about money or unnecessary financial worries.

- Be honest about what you can and can't afford. Follow through once you make commitments. Keep each other informed.
- Money management and financial responsibility are important life skills—you two are your children's primary teachers on money management.

Duty Parent: You are both 100% parents on duty per your residential schedule agreements. The duty parent is in charge and the decision maker on day-to-day decisions both at home and in public places with your children. Be respectful of your duty parent's role when interacting with the kids in public.

Guest Parent: There are times that you're both a part of activities for your children—whether that is a birthday party or a basketball game. Guest parent refers to the fact that you're welcome to attend, but not as a decision maker (unless you and your co-parent come to another mutually agreeable arrangement).

Project-Manager Parent: There will be events and activities that you will both want to be involved in. When your co-parenting relationship is strong, you will naturally and easily delegate tasks between you and things will work out smoothly. For many co-parents, this can be challenging. By assigning the role of project manager for a particular event, the parent who is taking the lead is responsible for flow, delegation, budgeting, and the overall project. This decreases confusion, competition and conflict.

- Events like shared holidays, birthday parties, or other celebrations are often assigned to one project-manager parent while the other is not only invited, but available to assist as requested.
- Large or complex school projects are often best overseen by one parent even as the child transitions back and forth between two homes. Again, coordination and complete and respectful communication is critical.

You may have other ideas for the business of co-parenting relationship that you design. There are many "co-" words that may be a good model for your situation: co-pilots, co-captains, co-lleagues, etc. What's important is that you find your way to a functional, business-like relationship that works for raising your kiddos!

Journal Moment 4

1. What do I want us to accomplish as co-parents?

_____

_____

_____

_____

2. Rather than fighting against each other for what's best for our kids, my co-parent and I will join forces and *fight for* the following to benefit our children:

_____

_____

_____

_____

_____

_____

_____

Co-Parenting Guiding Principles

Examples:

We want what is best for our kids.

I know they will do best if their other parent and I can work together on their behalf.

We don't want them to guess-and-stress about how to love each of us.

We want them to feel as safe and secure as possible through this transition of their family.

Here are my / our goals:

CHAPTER 5

Creating a Temporary Duty-Parent Schedule

Insight & Inspiration:

Suzy's Story...

It's a January morning in 2003 and I can't bring myself to take the kids to school. What will I say when someone asks me, "How are you?" The answer, you see, is just not the stuff of polite conversation.

W E L L... My partner of ten years has just dumped me. I was supposed to live with him into old age. He has dumped me with three kids under seven. With not enough savings to build a realistic future. With no job. With a house being sold to pay off debts I didn't know we had. With no pension. Even worse—I'm about to turn 40!

After ten years of learning to live with someone in love, it seemed so crazy just to give it all up because I now wanted to find a new way to live with him—albeit separately. I finally realized that posing "unanswerable questions" and re-examining the past *ad nauseam* were clearly not getting me anywhere. **I decided to let the love that had kept us together for ten years be the guiding factor in keeping us healthily and positively apart. The children were a constant reminder that anger and self-pity and doubt and fear—in other words, *parenthood*—can all be balanced with, well... love.**

I have learned that being with three young children, either in or out of a relationship, is not a chore or a burden. Even though it is hard sometimes, it does not stop me from living my life to the fullest. Parenthood, in any form, is a gift.

—**Suzy Miller** is your Alternative Divorce Guide, the creator of "Divorce in a Box" and "The Starting-Over Show." Suzy reaches people all over the world from the UK: www.startingovershow.com.

Creating a Temporary Duty-Parent Schedule

Duty parent simply refers to the parent in charge of the kids during a specified time: making decisions, caring for, preparing meals, managing behavior and discipline, and running the household during his / her duty-parent time. You are both always 100% parents, but as a family restructures from one home to two, and parents step away from the integrated parenting common in an intimate partnership, many adults find it helpful to begin to practice duty parenting.

By establishing predictable schedules of *who's-in-charge-when*, conflicts, competition and confusion often diminish. Each adult gets breathing room from the other during times when parenting together within the same household may be too difficult or too close for comfort. During those times when both parents are at home, the off-duty parent can consider him / herself as a guest and allow the duty parent full authority over the children and home.

Both parents may still be living in the family home or they may be nesting. The off-duty parent may choose to spend increasing amounts of time away from the family home. The children build familiarity with how parents will trade off one at a time to seamlessly love and care for them. Although this change requires adjustment, children quickly learn they have both of their parents in their lives with focus and predictability, and family life moves forward, often with less stress.

Your temporary duty-parent schedule is an opportunity to practice co-parenting. You will build trust with each other as you single-handedly manage the full range of child-care responsibilities. This can be a steep learning curve for one or both parents. Consider this among your first forays into developing a residential schedule—for now, it's a schedule on training wheels. This first experience gives you a runway to build proficiency and helps kids adjust to their up-coming two-home reality.

What is "Bird Nesting" and How Does it Work?

Have you ever watched bird parents come and go from the nest as they leave to retrieve food only to return to feed those wide-open mouths? This is what bird nesting is modeled after: one parent leaves the family home for a designated amount of time while the other stays back to care for the children, and then they trade—the other parent comes back to the family home and the current duty parent rotates out of the home on a pre-established schedule.

This model can be instrumental when parents recognize that continuing to live together for even a short period of time isn't working: the conflict is too high, the emotional loss and upset too disruptive. Rather than trying to make all the residential decisions quickly to get the needed adult separation, this temporary model can allow time for more thoughtful decision making while finances are sorted through without the additional stress of disrupting the children's lives.

Each parent may find an alternative place to stay when they are off duty, such as the home of a friend or family member. They may also decide to get a studio apartment for use by each parent when they are off duty. Of course, parents may have sufficient resources to have separate residences for each of them, while also maintaining the family home in which the children continue to reside. There are many potential options, and bird-nesting can be a positive step as you restructure your family and everyone adjusts to the change from parents to co-parents.

There are situations where longer-term bird nesting may be the best choice. When co-parents have a child whose needs are best served by not moving between two homes, or in fact, cannot tolerate the transitions. Large families may consider nesting if they determine that maintaining the family home meets everyone's needs better than two homes that can accommodate all the children with each parent.

Bird nesting requires a strong, constructive co-parenting relationship as well as roommate compatibility. We recommend that you work with a coach on how best to set up bird nesting whether in the short- or long-term. You will need house rules and agreements about everything from grocery shopping and laundry, to entertaining other adult guests in the family home or shared apartment (or similar).

Short-term nesting is generally followed with a more typical two-home family residential schedule and parenting plan. In long-term nesting, the desire to integrate new adult partner(s) or fatigue with the nesting arrangement for adults often brings everyone back to the table to discuss the viability of continuing to nest, or creating a new two-home option. We recommend that your parenting plan clearly articulate how this will be handled if / when either parent wishes to terminate bird nesting and begin a two-home arrangement.

How to Successfully Prepare for and Manage
Your Co-Parent Business Meetings

Like any well organized business meeting, you will want to set an agenda in advance.* One parent may be tasked with creating the initial agenda and submitting it to their co-parent for input and additions. Or, perhaps, both co-parents might exchange emails with the various issues they would like to discuss during the meeting and the agenda is crafted together from each party's emails. The intent is that each party should have a clear outline of the issues to be discussed during the co-parent business meeting. The location and length of the meeting should also be agreed upon.

Helpful tools for both parents to bring to the meeting include a paper version of a calendar, a notebook, and any other documentation that either parent may have with respect to child expenses to be discussed, enrollment forms for any school or extracurricular activities, and any other paperwork that supports any of the agenda items to be discussed.

A willingness to abide by the following ground rules will allow your meeting to be successful:

a) Listening carefully to each other's needs and interests;
b) Speaking respectfully to one another and limiting evaluation of each other's ideas;
c) Keeping your children central to the discussions and recognizing that they need both of you to be active and engaged in their lives.

As you make decisions, take good notes. Review notes with each other at the close of the meeting to confirm accuracy. It is often helpful if one parent is then responsible for crafting an email to the other parent recapping the decisions reached and any follow-up steps needed from that particular meeting. The receiving parent can check for accuracy and provide input for any changes that need to be made. The end result should be something similar to "meeting minutes" wherein both parents can look back and recall the discussion and agreements reached in case of the need for clarification in the future.

In addition to the above, homework for each parent can be assigned on any items yet to be resolved, along with the expected timeline for completion. Follow up conversations or meetings should be scheduled prior to adjourning. Perhaps you can schedule your next tri-annual business meeting so you will both be prepared when the time comes.

In the event you and your co-parent experience conflict or other strong emotions that interfere with your ability to communicate well, you might want to consider using a neutral professional to help you facilitate these meetings. Any experienced mediator, co-parent coach or family therapist trained in mediation would be excellent choices for providing that assistance. A neutral facilitator can help set the agenda, provide the safe venue for the dialogue, as well as assist you with note taking and providing a context within which you can capture your agreements and other decisions.

If you are unable to reach agreement, and there are important outstanding items that require agreement, you may decide to come back to the mediator for further assistance, consult your attorney for helpful advice, or initiate your conflict resolution provision in your parenting plan. Keep in mind that finding your way to resolution and maintaining your self-determination and co-parenting relationship has enormous value for your children.

*We have provided a template for creating your co-parent meeting agenda. See the next page.

Co-Parent Business Meeting Checklist
Guiding Co-Parents through the Planning Process

We encourage co-parents to meet at least three times each year: August for the first semester of school (Sept-Jan), again in January for the second semester of school (February—May), and in March for summer planning (June- August). The rhythms for your children and your work schedules will dictate the frequency and timing of your co-parent meetings. The template below is intended to help remind you of the essential areas of co-parenting to cover in each meeting.

School Schedule/Summer Schedule

- Planning for vacations, non-school days, holidays, camps, etc.
- Calendar parent—teacher conference dates
- Determine before and after school care
- Confirm agreement on extracurricular activities (including sports, arts, groups, etc.)
- Discuss bedtime—ensuring adequate rest
- Other

Academic Concerns

- Discuss tutoring, testing / evaluations, or consults with educational specialists
- Trouble-shoot homework issues
- Identify special projects for specific grade levels that need parental management and consider who will act as the project-manager parent
- Discuss electives: addressing class choices and managing equipment like musical instruments
- Other

Social Development

- Discuss peer relationships; exchange contact information for families involved in your children's lives as needed
- Anticipate developmental steps like sleepovers with friends, driving, starting to date, etc.
- Discuss any behaviors at either parent's home that are of concern
- Celebrate how wonderfully your child is growing
- Other

Physical Development

- Plan for primary care and dental care appointments
- Identify and discuss any other health care related issues
- Discuss and problem-solve any illness concerns / health management issues
- Assess self-care progression (diet, exercise, hygiene, etc)
- Other

Emotional Development

- Discuss self-esteem / self-confidence progression
- Consider how best to handle any mental health / anxiety-related concerns
- Develop strategies for behavior management concerns (angry outbursts?)
- Other

Household Changes

- Share information regarding changes in routines
- Share information if you are anticipating a move
- Share information if your are adding new family members (new pet, roommate, partnership)
- Share extended family news that impacts children
- Other

Journal Moment 5

1. What skills do I need to successfully fulfill my duty-parent role?

_____

_____

_____

_____

2. Which of these skills are best learned from my co-parent?

_____

_____

_____

_____

3. What other steps (books, classes, counseling) will I take to ensure I am ready to co-parent effectively?

_____

_____

_____

_____

VIDEO II
DESIGNING YOUR RESIDENTIAL SCHEDULE
Sharing Your Children Across Two Homes

Insight & Inspiration:

My Parents Had a Great Divorce...

As far as divorces go, my parents had a great one. Consequently, I grew up thinking divorce was a good thing.

After separating, my parents stopped fighting like a miserably married couple and began working together as dedicated members of a parenting team. At least, that was my adolescent observation. After a few years, they also regained a level of friendship which resulted in a few holiday dinners featuring both of my biological parents at the same table (treasure).

In the years following the divorce, I saw my family grow in ways I couldn't have imagined. As my parents re-coupled, I was happy to see them happy. I also found myself surrounded by a growing number of caring adults. I developed a friendship with my pseudo-stepsister that was so close we spent time together even when we were with our "other" parents.

I never felt the need to choose between homes. I didn't operate as a spy, nor was it necessary to refrain from discussing certain aspects of my life based on who I was with. I chatted happily with my mom's family about the time I spent with my dad, and vice versa. My new normal was, in many ways, more comfortable than the "normal" which preceded it.

These days I look back on that time with a combination of amazement and gratitude. As an adult, I'm constantly reminded of how lucky I was.

If you're reading this, I'm here to support you in creating a similar outcome for your children.

—**Tara Eisenhard** is the author of *The D-Word: Divorce Through a Child's Eyes*. She's a speaker; mediator and coach helping families achieve evolution over dissolution, **www.taraeisenhard.com**.

CHAPTER 6

Designing your Residential Schedule

Developmental Considerations

Insight & Inspiration:

"Can You Help Me Please? I'm Not Sure What's Going On..."

Try to resist the temptation to believe that as a good parent you ought to know exactly what's going on for your children. During your breakup, there's a lot they are probably keeping to themselves. They are frightened because they see you are, too. They wouldn't want to overburden you with their stuff, even if they were mature enough to know how to put it into words. In my experience, the really good parents are the ones who say *"Can you help me, please? - I'm not sure what's going on for my kids,"* rather than "Back off! - no-one knows my kids like I do!"

—**Christopher Mills** is a psychotherapist, mediator, family-law consultant, and author of *The Complete Guide to Divorced Parenting*. Chris practices in the UK. **www.chrismills.uk.com**

Model Healthy Relationships

Children's development doesn't depend on their parents being married or living together; what matters is that two parents (or more!) love their children and care enough to have healthy relationships with each other and with their children. Modeling healthy relationships over the long term is what really matters to children's development and success.

> —**Nicole Letourneau**, RN, PhD, FCAHS is a research professor at Alberta Children's Hospital Research Institute for Child & Maternal Health, University of Calgary, Alberta, Canada, and author of *Scientific Parenting: What Science Reveals About Parental Influence.*

What to Consider When Formulating a Daily Residential Schedule

You two are the best people to determine the residential schedule for your children, unless very unusual or complex circumstances exist. You may be wondering what considerations are important. Here are our recommendations:

- The developmental stages of your children help determine the frequency of contact and the length of time between contacts with each parent.

- For a very young child (under age three), ask yourselves: are both parents primary care-givers of the child—are you cultivating a primary bond with each parent? For older children, the availability of each parent to provide the nurture and care that children need for security and stability is considered.

- What is your child's temperament and how will that inform the frequency of contact with each parent and the capacity to tolerate transitions?

- Parents do not need to be identical in their child-rearing practices to be successful co-parents and raise resilient, well-adjusted children. However, if the discrepancy is too great, children spend an inordinate amount of energy adjusting to the differences between their parents, which can result in confusion, conflict, and disillusionment for children. A relatively shared view by parents on what children need is useful for kids.

- What is the nature of the conflict between you and your co-parent and how capable are you at managing conflict in a constructive manner?

- Are both of you capable-enough parents? Are there circumstances or conditions that impact good judgment, predictability, or the ability to utilize sound parenting skills? Can these be mitigated and if so, how?

- Does your child have special needs across any aspect of development? Are both of you capable of meeting those needs and have the necessary resources to meet the needs? If not yet, are you both willing to learn and fulfill what your child needs? Is your child able to tolerate transitions without undue duress?

- What is the geographic proximity of the two homes? Can both parents participate in the day-to-day logistics of the children's lives, school, extra-curricular activities, maintaining peer relationships, etc.?

As parents restructuring your family, you may find it difficult to sort out what are *your needs* from what are your *child's needs*. Reviewing "Qualities of a Good Divorce...What's Best for Kids" (found on page 6) along with the points listed above will help as you develop your residential schedule.

Including the Voices of Your Children in Your Parenting Plan

Parents often wonder how much "say" a child should have in their residential schedule. We land on the side that parents are the executive team of the family and consequently are the decision makers when it comes to the residential schedule and parenting planning. That said, children may have useful input regarding their hopes, needs, and concerns, which could benefit parents as they structure two-home family life. The children's input when sought by a skilled professional also can help clarify misperceptions held by either or both parents about what their children are *actually* needing and feeling.

Children rarely give parents accurate information—we call this "speaking to the choir." Kids don't want to say anything that might hurt either of their parents' feelings, or they may feel compelled to tell a parent what he / she wants to hear rather than what they actually think and feel. And, of course, each of your children may have very different thoughts and feelings that are lost unless individually addressed.

For older children, they may say mean and forceful opinions without any understanding of the long-term implications of what they're requesting or demanding. For very young children, they are likely to adopt a parent's thoughts and feelings—believing a parent is right and they must be wrong! We ask parents to be aware of this difficult quagmire when they start asking their kids to tell them what they want, or the even more difficult question, "Who do you want to live with?"

When parents have a similar view of their children, we typically trust their knowing and their confidence that they are making good decisions for their children's schedule and two-home family (unless something most unusual or unskillful is being considered). When parents are contentious about their kids' needs, or have a radically different view about a residential schedule, we recommend utilizing a child specialist to further explore the children's perception of home life, relationship with each parent, and developmental appropriateness of scheduling options.

A child specialist is trained for interviewing children as their family is restructured and parents navigate divorce. Unlike a child therapist who has confidentiality guidelines and ethical considerations limiting how they help parents with residential schedules, the child specialist is free to share the information gleaned from the children with the parents for the purpose of understanding *what's working and what's hurting* for each of the children. The child specialist is trained in growth and development and in family systems undergoing change. This can be one of the best ways for parents to get help with their parenting planning when their views of their children or their intentions over the residential schedule create conflict.

Journal Moment 6

1. What growth and developmental considerations do I want to incorporate into designing our residential schedule?

_____

_____

_____

_____

_____

2. What other important considerations matter to me as I think about my children expanding their sense of family across two homes?

_____

_____

_____

_____

_____

CHAPTER 7

Residential Schedules for School-age Children

Insight & Inspiration:

Resting into "Enough Time" with Your Kids...

Kids don't count hours or overnights. They don't want to feel like a possession that needs to be divided up. They just want to have a stress-free relationship with each of their parents.

Focus on enjoying the parenting time you have with your children. When you do this, your children sense that you trust the strength of your relationship with them and you support their relationship with their other parent. They don't need to worry about your needs and feelings—they just get to feel loved and cared for. They get to be kids focusing on their lives and relationships without undue concern.

We burden kids with balancing the scales of time when we underscore and compete for hours, days and overnights—when they hear language like "I'm getting *my time* and you're...." When children feel the burden and stress about parents having enough time with them, they feel helpless. Over time, they develop resentment; begin caretaking adults rather than enjoying their carefree childhood. Often they do all three: resent, care-take, and lose their carefree childhood.

When you let go of competition, and accept and rest into building your new sense of rhythm and relationship with your children, everyone can relax and enjoy the growing stability of two-home family life.

—**Lisa Gabardi**, Ph.D., author of *The Quick Guide to Co-Parenting After Divorce: Three Steps to Your Children's Healthy Adjustment*, is in private practice in Beaverton, Oregon, **www.gabardi.com**

Utilize the Proper Parenting Plan
for Your Jurisdiction

This next section of the Workbook provides worksheets for you and your co-parent to write agreements for each of the sections commonly found in parenting plans. However, there is not a uniform parenting plan document used in all jurisdictions. You will want to determine the proper form or court pleading that has been adopted where you will be filing your legal action with the court. The parenting plan worksheets in the workbook can be easily adopted into whatever form your jurisdiction requires.

If you do not know the proper parenting plan form utilized in your jurisdiction, you can easily locate it by re-searching online through your local or state court's website under family law forms, asking for assistance from the clerk in your local law library, or consulting with an attorney, who should be able to make that form available to you. Please note that the parenting plan worksheets contained in this Workbook are for you to use for drafting and discussion purposes with your co-parent—THEY ARE NOT CONSIDERED TO BE A LEGAL PLEADING in and of themselves. In other words, the purpose of these worksheets is to provide the foundation for crafting language you or your attorney will then convert to the appropriate format or parenting plan document utilized in your juris-diction.

Remember: your parenting plan is a legal document; we strongly recommend you review your parenting plan agreements with an attorney to fully understand the legal implications of your planning decisions.

"The River" or Rhythm of a Daily Residential Schedule

Children benefit from rhythms and predictability. Predictability and planning diminishes conflict for co-parents. The daily residential schedule provides children and adults much needed security about how the children's activities will flow and parenting duties will be fulfilled. When we allow the daily residential schedule river to flow underneath any and all schedule exceptions, we always know how to accommodate an exception and return to the established schedule, rather than allowing any one exception to change the course of the river —which runs the risk of disrupting future plans downstream.

When we have an established every other weekend schedule, this can be very helpful. Co-parents can plan weeks, months, even years ahead for child-free weekends, or weekends with the children doing special events without impacting the co-parent's schedule. We may need to swap a weekend from time to time, and we simply return to the schedule as it would have been prior to the swap. We think of the schedule exception as jumping up onto the bank temporarily out of schedule, only to jump back into the river once the exception has been taken care of—long term schedule unchanged.

Here is an example of how swapping weekends are managed while maintaining the river.

> Kurt was invited up to a friend's cabin with the kids for a whale watching expedition. The dates fell on his co-parent's weekend. Kurt approached Sarah about swapping a weekend so that he might be able to accept the offer. Sarah was happy to make the swap. Kurt took Sarah's residential weekend and she requested Kurt's weekend preceding the cabin trip in exchange. That worked for Kurt. This resulted in Sarah having the kids two weekends in a row, and Kurt also getting two weekends in a row. Then they returned to their regularly scheduled weekend rhythm—Sarah on her regularly scheduled weekend and Kurt back to his.

Right of First Refusal

Requiring your co-parent to offer you time with the children during ongoing, residential time can create an atmosphere of feeling controlled by a co-parent. Not surprising, this loss of autonomy often builds resentment.

When co-parents are getting along, offering the children to one another in their absence comes naturally and easily. We call this *generosity*. When co-parents have a strained and difficult relationship, being forced to offer the kids back-and-forth during residential time is a set up for unnecessary strain for everyone involved. Like it or not, it is a set-up for game playing with time—a game no one wins.

Remember: your children benefit from a variety of child-care experiences which happen routinely in day-to-day life that don't always involve a parent. Grandparents come to visit. Sleepovers with a friend's family may be a natural option. The chance to have McKenzie come over and baby-sit becomes a weekend bonus.

Limit any use of Right of First Refusal to those situations where it makes sense. Some parents agree that overnights away from the children would be a time for implementing the Right of First Refusal. Others build in exceptions for grandparent or immediate family care-givers. If you're concerned about romantic partners functioning as parent substitutes, then set those boundaries rather than utilizing Right of First Refusal in a way that creates conflict.

In the face of so much loss early in your separation, requiring your co-parent to offer *any available time* with your children can feel essential. However, over time and with adjustment, the ability to make decisions that fit the situation may be much more important to both you and your co-parent.

"Generosity is the flower of justice."

—Nathaniel Hawthorne

Journal Moment 7

1. How will I reconcile the loss of time with my child—how will I accept less than 100% parenting?

_____

_____

_____

_____

_____

2. What is it that I know our children learn from having time with each of us? How will I reconcile the loss of time with my child—how will I accept less parenting while valuing my kids' relationship with their other parent?

_____

_____

_____

_____

_____

Daily Residential / Parenting Schedule

For examples of residential schedules, please go to the Addenda:
On-Line Resources for Residential Schedule Patterns, pg 122.

INFANT/PRESCHOOL SCHEDULE

☐ Identify the specific times that each parent will be "on duty" with the child.

☐ Identify the parent's residence in which the child will be sleeping overnight for each day of the week (keeping in mind the non-residential parent may have "duty times" to care for an infant or very young child even if overnights have not yet begun, or continue to be limited to a weekend, for example.)

☐ Use the provided templates for the tiers as you build a developmentally appropriate progression in residential time for your little one. You may want or need more—please just expand to what you need!

☐ Provide the dates for the beginning of each tier's schedule and the end of each tier's schedule.

TIER 1 Begins _____ **and ends** _____ **(specify dates)**

WEEK ONE

	Sunday	Monday	Tuesday	Wed	Thursday	Friday	Saturday
Morning							
Afternoon							
Evening							
Overnight							

WEEK TWO

	Sunday	Monday	Tuesday	Wed	Thursday	Friday	Saturday
Morning							
Afternoon							
Evening							
Overnight							

Special notes or considerations:

_____

_____

_____

_____

*For examples of residential schedules, please go to the Addenda: On-Line Resources for Residential Schedule Patterns, pg 122.

TIER 2 Begins _____ **and ends** _____ **(specify dates)**

WEEK ONE

	Sunday	Monday	Tuesday	Wed	Thursday	Friday	Saturday
Morning							
Afternoon							
Evening							
Overnight							

WEEK TWO

	Sunday	Monday	Tuesday	Wed	Thursday	Friday	Saturday
Morning							
Afternoon							
Evening							
Overnight							

Weekend Rhythms/Scheduling: If your residential schedule evolves to include an every-other-weekend pattern, be sure to maintain that underlying rhythm—that is your "river" or rhythm underneath all the other exceptions that might come up when school breaks and holidays are introduced. Rather than resetting your weekend schedule to accommodate breaks and holidays, simply return to the river. That way you will be able to predict your duty weekends and your child-free weekends for years to come!

Special notes or considerations:

_____

_____

_____

_____

_____

_____

_____

_____

TIER 3 Begins _____ **and ends** _____ **(specify dates)**

WEEK ONE

	Sunday	Monday	Tuesday	Wed	Thursday	Friday	Saturday
Morning							
Afternoon							
Evening							
Overnight							

WEEK TWO

	Sunday	Monday	Tuesday	Wed	Thursday	Friday	Saturday
Morning							
Afternoon							
Evening							
Overnight							

Special notes or considerations:

_____

_____

_____

_____

_____

_____

_____

RESIDENTIAL SCHEDULE FOR SCHOOL-AGE CHILDREN

☐ Identify the specific times that each parent will be on duty with the children.

☐ Identify the parent's residence in which the children will be sleeping overnight for each day of the week (keeping in mind the non-residential parent may have duty times during the residential parent's time.)

☐ We have provided templates for two tiers as you build a developmentally appropriate residential schedule for your growing school-age children. You may want / need more—please just expand to what you need!

☐ Provide the dates for the beginning of the schedule and end of the schedule.

TIER 1 Begins _____ and ends _____ (specify dates)

WEEK ONE

	Sunday	Monday	Tuesday	Wed	Thursday	Friday	Saturday
Morning							
Afternoon							
Evening							
Overnight							

WEEK TWO

	Sunday	Monday	Tuesday	Wed	Thursday	Friday	Saturday
Morning							
Afternoon							
Evening							
Overnight							

Special notes or considerations:

_____

_____

_____

_____

_____

_____

_____

TIER 2 Begins _____ **and ends** _____ **(specify dates)**

WEEK ONE

	Sunday	Monday	Tuesday	Wed	Thursday	Friday	Saturday
Morning							
Afternoon							
Evening							
Overnight							

WEEK TWO

	Sunday	Monday	Tuesday	Wed	Thursday	Friday	Saturday
Morning							
Afternoon							
Evening							
Overnight							

Weekend Rhythms/Scheduling: If your residential schedule evolves to include an every-other-weekend pattern, be sure to maintain that underlying rhythm—that is your "river" or rhythm underneath all the other exceptions that might come up when school breaks and holidays are introduced. Rather than resetting your weekend schedule to accommodate breaks and holidays, simply return to the river. That way you will be able to predict your duty weekends and your child-free weekends for years to come!

Special notes or considerations:

_____

_____

_____

_____

_____

_____

_____

_____

Insight & Inspiration:

Strong Co-Parenting is Good for Your Kids' Health...

As a school nurse, many kids come to my office with health complaints, which are often the result of stressful circumstances at home. When co-parenting is not going well, children suffer and health complaints increase. When parents take the time to build and follow a good Parenting Plan, diminish conflict between homes and maintain enough cooperation between them, I see happy, well-adjusted children succeeding at school. When these kids are stopping by my office, it's just an excuse to miss class and come by and say "hi" ...kids being kids. Your work as co-parents makes a difference!

—**Wendi Schuller** is a nurse, and author of *The Global Guide to Divorce*, published by Austin Macauley, London, October, 2015
www.globalguidetodivorce.com

CHAPTER 8

Summer Vacation and Vacations with Parents

Insight & Inspiration:

Make Summer Fun...

"How can parents in two home families make a kid's summer fun?"

1. I can play with my friends
2. Let me see my other parent after trips
3. Both come to my soccer game
4. I get to talk to my other parent about fun whenever I want!!!!!!!

— Sebastian W., age 8

How to Manage Conflicting Priorities

Sometimes you will find that your designated residential schedule for school breaks may overlap particular holidays, or a preferred vacation time may overlap with a special occasion. When anticipating how to resolve a conflict in scheduling, it is important for you and your co-parent to consider how you value each of the days in question. In other words, what does a religious holiday such as Christmas or Passover mean to each of you and to the children? Do you value the freedom to travel during school breaks over limitations imposed by holiday celebrations? Do vacations with parents during the summer have more importance than a child's summer birthday or recognized holiday?

If you and your co-parent remain flexible and maintain good communication, conflicts over important days inadvertently caused by your residential schedule can be mitigated without confusion or duress. If you and your co-parent have conducted regular business meetings, you will have anticipated conflicts in the schedule in advance and resolved them.

Along with considering how you and the children value particular days, know that you can also "horse trade" days or overnights with your co-parent to allow the children's schedule to run more smoothly and allow both of you to get your agendas honored. For example, your co-parent has a special opportunity to take the children on a camping trip over July 4th, and that happens to be a holiday assigned to you this year. Is there another holiday or special weekend that would allow you to offer your July 4th holiday in trade? Being flexible with one another and focusing on facilitating good experiences for your children while respecting each other's time with the children will pay off big dividends in the future with respect to rebuilding trust and expanding opportunities for both you and your children.

Note: In Chapter 17 we will cover "Establishing Priorities" for your residential schedule. When co-parents can't agree on resolving the inevitable conflicts that emerge, the priority list will ultimately resolve the conflict and establish who has priority for what days.

Journal Moment 8

1. What made summer special for me as a child?

_____

_____

_____

_____

_____

2. How will I incorporate opportunities for special summer experiences into our parenting plan?

_____

_____

_____

_____

_____

Summer Schedule

Examples / options:

A. Children will reside with the parents according to the school residential schedule during the summer vacation from school.

B. The children will begin a new school residential schedule as outlined in this parenting plan beginning the first Monday of August.

C. The children will reside with the parents using the following schedule during the weeks of summer break beginning the first Monday after the release from school until the last Friday prior to school restarting.

SUMMER: Begins _____ at _____ AM/PM and ends _____ at _____ AM/PM

WEEK ONE

	Sunday	Monday	Tuesday	Wed	Thursday	Friday	Saturday
Morning							
Afternoon							
Evening							
Overnight							

WEEK TWO

	Sunday	Monday	Tuesday	Wed	Thursday	Friday	Saturday
Morning							
Afternoon							
Evening							
Overnight							

Special notes:

_____

_____

_____

_____

_____

_____

_____

Summer Vacations with Parents

Examples/options:

A. Each parent will have one / two / three vacation(s) during the summer of up to (X) consecutive overnights each including the parent's regular residential time.

B. Each parent may have up to a total of 14 (or X) overnights of vacation with the children taken in up to two blocks including the parent's regular residential time.

C. Each parent will have one seven-night vacation with the children and will have one seven-night vacation without the children. Each parent agrees to provide childcare for the other parent during his / her child-free vacation arranged by mutual agreement.

What would you suggest for summer vacation durations with each parent?

_____

_____

_____

_____

- Vacation will commence at _____ AM/PM on the first day of vacation and end at _____ AM/PM on the last day unless otherwise agreed upon.

Vacation Durations Grow with Children: You can create increasing lengths of vacations in steps / tiers just like the residential schedule. What makes sense for a five-year-old may be too limited for a 12-year-old! Would you like to specify a different vacation allowance for each parent at some point in the future?

_____

_____

_____

_____

The following guidelines are proposed for your consideration:

☐ **Priority for Choosing Vacation:** The parents will inform each other during their March planning meeting and no later than March 31st (choose date) of their summer vacation plans. In the event of a conflict, the mother / parent will have priority for choosing her vacation in the "odd years" and the father / other parent will have priority in the "even years". If the parents are taking multiple vacations, they will take turns choosing their first and then their second, etc.

☐ **Resolving Disputes in a Timely Manner:** Any open questions or differences of opinion concerning the summer schedule will be addressed directly between the parents during their March planning meeting, and in any event no later than March 31st. If they are unsuccessful in reaching agreement on the summer schedule, they will initiate their chosen dispute resolution process no later than April 10th.

☐ **Late Requests:** Vacations requested after March 31st will be considered but will require mutual agreement to move forward.

☐ **Extended Vacation:** Each parent may request one / two (or more) extended summer vacations of up to 28 overnights with the children during the life of this parenting plan. The vacation notification must be given no later than March 31st of the year of travel.

Travel Guidelines

The following guidelines are proposed for your consideration. Some may apply to your parenting plan, others will not. Your legal team can assist you.

☐ **Travel Out of the Area for Overnights:** The parents agree to provide each other basic information such as travel dates, times, and means of transportation (flight numbers if appropriate) when traveling with the children away from home and spending the night out of the area. Parents agree to provide the other with alternative contact information if cell coverage is limited or unavailable for cases of emergency.

☐ **Children's Passport/Travel:** If the parents agree to obtain passports for the children, the parents shall cooperate in obtaining and renewing the passports when necessary and share the related costs. The parent who last travels with the children shall hold the passports until the other parent needs them to travel with the children. A parent traveling out of the country with the children shall be provided with their passports and any other necessary forms or travel authorizations no later than two weeks prior to the date of travel.

☐ **International Travel:** A parent shall not travel with the children outside of the (insert your home country) without the written permission of the other parent, which permission shall not be unreasonably withheld. Any parent wishing to travel internationally with the children must advise the other parent in writing (X time) in advance, providing a proposed itinerary and contact information for each day out of country.

Other Summer Planning Considerations

Do you have family reunions, annual events, or similar experiences that you want to protect for your children and specifically identify in the parenting plan?

_____

_____

_____

☐ **Prioritizing Children's Summer Experiences:** The parents agree that summer camps (name experiences if something specific, i.e. "swim team participation") are important for their children, and will be flexible with the summer schedule so the children can attend appropriate activities. However, neither parent will enroll a child in a summer camp or other activity that interferes with the other parent's residential time without that parent's agreement.

☐ **Balancing the Summer Schedule:** In the event that vacations with parents, special events, and other children's activities, create an imbalance within the children's rhythm for residential time with each parent, the parents will work together to bring some element of rhythm / balance back into the weeks of summer break, respecting the children's needs for contact with each parent in reasonable intervals.

As children get older, they have increasing opportunities to be away from home during the summer at sleep-away camps, internship or other learning / volunteer experiences, and their own work schedules, which impact your residential time. Our first job as parents is to facilitate these experiences for our children. Our second job is to look at the schedule and create opportunities for the child to see each parent when returning home after extended leave. Your parenting plan can not anticipate all the different life experiences you'll face with your children or guarantee good co-parenting judgment for both of you. You can only do your best when the time comes to create a positive co-parenting atmosphere and family life for children.

CHAPTER 9

Scheduling School Breaks

Insight & Inspiration:

Your Desire for Peace is Greater than Your Desire to be "Right"...

Learning to cooperate with your children's other parent does not always mean agreement; it does not always mean that you have good feelings toward that other parent. It means that your love and care for your child is stronger than your anger and sadness, and your desire for peace is greater than your desire to be "right".

—**Kristin Little**, MA, MS, LMHC is the contributing author of *The Co-Parents' Handbook*, counselor and a Collaborative Law Child Specialist in the greater Seattle area: **www.kristinlittlecounseling.com**

School Breaks Offer Another Option
for Travel or Stay-cation

When developing your parenting plan, specify whether "vacation with children" includes travel during school breaks or whether vacation with children designates travel only during the extended summer vacation from school. Most parents understand that school breaks offer an additional window of time for travel that is not restricted or limited, but rather, in addition to "vacation with children."

Just as a parent may travel over their residential weekend for a trip to the grandparents or camping trip, parents may use their designated residential time during a school break for travel or stay-cation; we recommend that you clarify with each other to ensure you both have a shared understanding of vacation time and options to travel during school breaks.

Stay-cation refers to taking time off from work to be with the children without out-of-town travel—staying home for your vacation.

"Look at me! Look at me! Look at me NOW!
It is fun to have fun, but you have to know how."

—Dr. Seuss

Journal Moment 9

1. How will my work schedule, vacation time, and child care needs impact my parenting planning when considering how to designate school breaks?

_____

_____

_____

_____

2. Do I want to create an option for travel or stay-cation if I otherwise generally intend to follow the residential schedule during these times?

_____

_____

_____

_____

School Breaks
Including Winter Vacation

Check all school breaks that apply (separate section on Winter Vacation follows):

☐ Fall Break

☐ Mid-Winter Break

☐ Spring Break

☐ Other: _____

In creating a break schedule, you will:

☐ Identify the break by name

☐ Define when the break begins and ends (use specific days and times)

☐ Determine how you will share time with the children for that particular break.

- Will we rotate odd / even years or does one parent have a preference for one break and the other parent for another break every year?
- Will we preserve our regularly scheduled weekends when breaks are a full week off from school—the break is limited to the days off from school along with our adjacent residential weekend?
- When we include both weekends as part of the break, will we swap weekends to avoid one parent having three weekends in a row?
- Will we divide the breaks in half instead of rotating? What will be our transition day and time?
- Will the children maintain their regular school schedule during the break?
- If following the regular residential schedule makes the most sense generally, will we create an option for a parent to travel or take time off from work during a break to spend with the children when that's possible?
- Have we clearly labeled transition days and times? Do transitions allow for smooth flow out of and back into school residential time for the children?

Here are examples of possible options for school breaks:

A. Children will reside with the parents according to the school residential schedule during the (name of the break) from school.

B. For the (name the break), the children will reside with one parent (mother) in the even years and with the other parent (father) in the odd years. The break will be defined as the days off from school and the parent's regularly scheduled adjacent weekend.*

C. The children will reside with the parents on the following schedule for the (name the break and follow with the specific overnights of break with each parent and the time of transition).

*For week-long breaks, define the times that the break begins and ends in such a way that the parent's residential weekend flows naturally with the school break. This presumes an every other weekend schedule and will be addressed differently if your schedule involves splitting every weekend.

Creating rhythms: Generally speaking, parents often create a rhythm with the school breaks that rotates back and forth over the school year. For example: If one parent gets mid-winter break this year, the other gets spring break. Next year, you will swap, which allows each of you to experience each break every other year.

Choosing beginning and ending transition times: As a practice, try and use the same transition times for beginning and ending breaks and holidays. Having predictable transition times can make things much easier to track and remember for both parents and kids.

Here are other possible ways to structure school breaks:

D. (For week-long breaks.) Children will reside with the parents according to the school residential schedule during the (name of the break) from school unless the parent with priority for travel / stay-cation wishes to exercise their priority to have extended time with the children. One parent (the mother) has priority to travel / stay-cation in the odd years and the other parent (father) in the even years. The travel / stay-cation parent will give the other parent 60 days notice if planning to exercise his / her priority to spend the break with the children. Travel will not disrupt regularly scheduled weekend time unless by agreement.

E. The (name the break), begins when school releases and ends when school resumes. In the event that this results in three weekends in a row with one parent, the parents will swap either the weekend before or the weekend after by mutual agreement. If they are unable to agree, they will swap the weekend before. (This is often a preference when a parent plans to travel longer distances during a school break.)

F. (When a break is less than a week long.) The (name break) begins when school releases and ends when school resumes**. One parent (the mother) will have priority in odd years and the other parent (father) will have priority in even years. If this results in three weekends in a row....*add language if you want to build in a weekend swap.**

Winter Vacation

Winter Vacation is the longest of the school year breaks in our area and includes the special winter holidays. Consequently, we often talk about it separately and pay attention to its uniqueness.

Typical questions parents ask:

- Will we schedule the break time and celebrate the holidays one way for the first couple of years after separation and schedule the break differently long term?

- Will we divide the break in some way? In half? Will this be our long-term strategy?

- Will we follow the school residential schedule? Should this be our short-term strategy and simply celebrate the holidays, keeping things simple at first?

- Will we carve out a certain number of days for travel and rotate that option each year—one of us in odd years and the other in even? If we do that, will the other days follow the school residential schedule?

- Are there particular rituals / traditions that we want to honor—at least every other year for each of us? What are they and how can we define the schedule in a way that best supports those rituals / traditions for each of us with our children?

- Do we want to consider extended family? If one of our siblings has his / her children in even years for Christmas, is that something we want to accommodate so the cousins can get together during break?

Once a parent has requested a break for travel / stay-cation and the other parent has accepted the request, a reversal back to residential schedule or any other scheduling change happens by mutual agreement. Once schedule changes are announced and acknowledged, the schedule is confirmed and cannot be reversed without agreement. Because your co-parent is free to make alternative plans, expecting your co-parent to change plans simply because your plans have changed is not reasonable unless by agreement.

---

* You may prefer to use literal days and times, for example, Friday at 6 PM or Saturday at 10 AM, which are unrelated to the school start and stop times and more consistent with your typical transition times based on childcare or other preferences.

Whatever you two decide, you will want to define the vacation / break. Winter Vacation begins (you choose your times):

- At 5 PM on the day released from school, or
- At 9 AM on the day following release from school

...and ends:

- Upon return to school (9 AM), or
- At 7 PM (your normal transition time) the evening prior to return to school

When dividing the break in half:

- Determine which parent will have the first half and which will have the second half and whether you will rotate that each year.*
- In the event that Winter Vacation has an odd number of overnights, specify that the "extra overnight" shall be added to the first-half/second half (choose).
- Unless otherwise agreed upon, the transition time shall be at (choose time) on the later of December 26 or the mid-point day of Winter Vacation (this ensures that Christmas will fall in the first half of the break).
- Consider whether travel during the break will have priority over any contact with the children for the holiday. (We will be covering holiday scheduling with you in the next chapter.) For example, if one of you wants to take the children to the grandparents for Christmas and you're scheduled to have the children for the first half of break, but you've scheduled to split the Christmas holiday with your co-parent, traveling over Christmas will result in conflict over celebrating the holiday—the children can't be in two places at once. You will have to prioritize either the school break schedule or the holiday schedule to determine which holds higher importance. (We cover establishing priorities in Chapter 17.)

Special note: you may not care about celebrating the holidays right now or you may feel generous and want to offer the holiday celebrations to your co-parent in these first couple of years. Long term, you may not want to miss every holiday season with your children. Remember your circumstances are likely to change and kids benefit from holiday experiences with both parents.

When choosing a travel window between the holidays:

Sometimes parents prefer to create an option to travel between 12/26–12/30, and rotate the option to travel every-other-year during, which prevents conflict with holiday celebrations. This can preserve the option to share holiday time with the children either together or in tandem when possible. Be sure you:

- Clearly identify when travel may begin and when the children are expected to return to the residential schedule.
- Know what the schedule is prior to travel and what it will be after travel.
- Do your best to make the children's transition out of their school schedule into whatever the Winter Vacation schedule may be (including holidays) and back into their school schedule as seamless as possible. This may require some adjusting once you look at the calendar each year and see how the break actually maps with your scheduling guidelines and plans.
- Keep in mind, if conflict ensues, what you have written in your parenting plan prevails.

SCHOOL BREAKS

School Breaks	Defined as (start time/ end time)	Describe how the children will spend time with parent(s)	Odd	Even	Every

Special notes on other celebrations to be included in your parenting plan:

CHAPTER 10

Scheduling Holidays
and Celebrations

Holidays are a Time of Tradition

...and with a divorce, your family's traditions are going to change. Be realistic about the holidays. Letting go of old traditions can be sad; creating new ones can be both hard and exciting. Perhaps you and your co-parent will work together to preserve some traditions together for your children. Either way, in time, you will discover new ways to create satisfying celebrations, rituals and traditions.

Remember that with a little creativity, you can make *any day* a holiday. So try to be flexible when rotating the *exact day* of a holiday. If your co-parent wants to take the kids away for the entire Christmas holiday to visit his or her parents and siblings who live two states away, think twice before screaming "No!" (Although you may *feel* just that way.)

Ask yourself whether the annual Christmas road trip to the grandparents is a tradition that you want your children to lose forever? Maybe this year your kids go with your co-parent, and next year you can start a new tradition— you begin a holiday adventure with them yourself that begins to build memories that endure.

Is all of this optimal? No. Is it the way it *should* be? That depends on your expectations of what should and shouldn't be. The most important thing to remember, though, is that holidays are a time for celebration. The worst thing you can do is make what should be a happy time for children into a battleground between adults that ruins the holiday for *everyone*.

> —**Karen Covy** is a divorce attorney, advisor, and author of *When Happily Ever After Ends: How to Survive Your Divorce Emotionally, Financially and Legally.* She practices in Chicago: **www.karencovy.com**

"It is tenderness for the past, courage for the present, hope for the future.
It is a fervent wish that every cup may overflow with blessings rich and eternal,
and that every path may lead to peace."

—Agnes M. Pharo

Journal Moment 10

1. What are the holidays and rituals I would like to preserve?

_____

_____

_____

_____

_____

2. How can I preserve them while honoring my co-parent's desire to also have important holiday experiences with our children?

_____

_____

_____

_____

_____

3. How will I ensure my children get to relax, settle, and enjoy their holidays with a parent without feeling torn, rushed or pulled in too many directions?

_____

_____

_____

_____

_____

Holidays

Most parenting plans will consider major holidays and provide options for including other family-specific holidays. You may choose which to celebrate based on your traditions, religion, and ethnicity. There may be holidays in your court-mandated form that are unimportant to you; you may choose to designate those holidays as part of the reg-ular residential schedule. Holidays create an *option* for parents to create a schedule exception, not a requirement to disrupt the children's daily schedule when a holiday holds no particular importance in your family.

To prepare for your holiday scheduling, you will want to:

- Look at the list of suggested holidays that is part of your court-mandated form.

- Which of those holidays are important to you and your co-parent to celebrate outside of the regular residential schedule? (This generally means that you want to rotate or share them in some way to ensure that you both have an opportunity to experience the holiday with your children.)

- Which holidays are missing from the list that you both know are important to your children's sense of family and tradition? Can you add them? (For example, Christmas is the only religious holiday listed in our court-mandated form in Washington state. Others must be added if parents want them acknowledged and scheduled outside the regular schedule.)

- Which holidays will be celebrated or acknowledged by the residential parent without making a change to the schedule? These can be labeled, "Per regular residential schedule".

- Which holidays are often part of a long weekend? (In the US, those would be Monday holidays like Memorial Day and Labor Day.)

- And, lastly, which holidays occur during a school break?

(Keep in mind we'll talk about Special Occasions separately.)

Breaking holidays into two parts: Parents often wonder if children should see each parent at every holiday. (Many parents want to be sure they get to see their children at every holiday). This may be very helpful in the first year or two while everyone adjusts. Beyond the short term, asking children to be in two different locations every holiday—leaving one celebration in the middle and entering another that is often in progress—can be distressing. Over time, consider allowing your child to rest into a full holiday experience with one or the other of you for any given holiday and rotate from year to year who has the opportunity to share that particular family experience with the children.

Scheduling holidays that are part of a school break: Generally, parents make every effort to match the assign-ment of a holiday with the assignment of the overlapping school break. A potential example is assigning Easter (or Passover) with the parent who is also assigned Spring Break. If the holiday and break "overlap," there won't be a conflict between the parent celebrating Spring Break and the other parent celebrating the holiday.

Holidays that may fall near a weekend: You have a few options when these long weekend holidays occur. You may want to define the holiday as the entire weekend. Be sure to identify start and stop times adequately to avoid confusion and allow for smooth transitions out of and back into the residential schedule. You may want to rotate those year to year so that each of you can enjoy the long weekend experiences. If the holiday schedule falls in such a way that it creates three weekends in a row with one parent, you can opt to swap the weekend be-fore or after the holiday weekend—giving each parent two weekends in a row instead of one parent having three weekends in a row. Other options include: celebrating the holiday as the day (or portion of a day) or as a single overnight, or simply attaching the holiday to whomever has the residential weekend—allowing that parent the three-day weekend by default.

(Don't forget the value of maintaining your long-term every-other-weekend schedule, "the river." See Chapter 7 for review.)

HOLIDAY LIST

Holiday	Defined as (start time / end time)	Children with which parent (Mom / Dad)	Odd	Even	Every

Special notes on other celebrations to be included in your parenting plan:

_____

_____

_____

CHAPTER 11

Scheduling Special Occasions

Insight & Inspiration:

Respecting Your Child's Relationships with Others...

The obligation of a parent is to the child and includes respecting all the relationships of the child, even if one parent cannot respect the other. As we respect the relationships of the child, the child internalizes a sense of value and worth, key ingredients toward the development of their self esteem. By respecting the relationships of the child, we are also less likely to find ourselves in conflict with the child's extended kin with whom we may take exception. So the challenge is often advancing the relationships of the child ahead of the parent's feelings toward those people who we may otherwise now seek to be separate from. Even in view of concerns, the challenge remains to find ways to keep the child's relationships intact.

Children will come to learn by virtue of their own experience, the nature of the relatives. Let them come to learn firsthand, lest they begrudge you, believing you have participated in thwarting a relationship in your own interest—not theirs. Be there to provide support and encouragement in the event that their life experience teaches that some relationships are more wholesome and giving than others. As we support our children through their life's journey, we then become a respected and valued parent and we increase the likelihood of our children seeking our guidance and being open to our influence.

—**Gary Direnfeld**, MSW, RSW, is a social worker, media personality, author, parenting columnist and speaker in Ontario, Canada, **www.yoursocialworker.com**.

The Value of an "Old-Fashioned" Calendar

Work with a paper or laminated calendar when you make your parenting schedule—preferably one that has all of the major holidays on it. Working with a calendar while you are creating your residential schedule can help you visualize exactly what that schedule will look like in a way that nothing else can. (Marking your time and your co-parent's time in separate colors also helps you instantly see where the schedule gets bumpy for the kids and / or *just won't work*.)

Remember when making your schedule, your kids don't want to spend their entire childhood in a car, being driven back and forth between their two homes! Find the right balance between time with each parent and having kids move between households—keeping in mind their developmental needs.

Mark your calendar with school breaks, days-off, holidays, important events, and special occasions. It is very easy to forget about some of these special opportunities with kids when you have a thousand other things on your mind! You don't have to divvy up every conceivable special opportunity (although some parents do); you also don't want to overlook something that is important to you, your co-parent, or your kids.

—**Karen Covy** is a divorce attorney, advisor, and author of *When Happily Ever After Ends: How to Survive Your Divorce Emotionally, Financially and Legally*. She practices in Chicago: **www.karencovy.com**

Journal Moment 11

1. What are the traditions around birthdays and other special days that I want to preserve?

_____

_____

_____

_____

_____

2. What aspects of those occasions do I want to document in our parenting plan?

_____

_____

_____

_____

_____

Special Occasions

Here you'll be addressing Mother's Day / Father's Day, birthdays, and other special occasions that are important in your family. By now, you've become familiar with:

- Defining the occasion (when does it start and when does it end?)

- Examining how the special occasion fits into the children's ongoing residential schedule—thinking about transitions into the special occasion and back out into the regular residential schedule to avoid bumpiness or awkward amounts of time between transitions.

- And lastly, have you considered whether a schedule change is required to mark the special occasion—or perhaps a visit with the non-residential parent will suffice?

Occasion	With?	Start and End Times
Mother's Day		
Father's Day		
Birthdays		
Others		

(Mother's / Father's Day need to be designated differently when we have parents who are either two moms or two dads.)

Since these special occasions fall on Sundays, they may occur on your regular residential time if you are rotating weekends. If they fall on your co-parent's residential time, you get to decide how to modify the schedule so that your children can celebrate with you. You can celebrate "childfree" if that's what either of you prefer. Your definition of this special parent day can be unique to each of you. Typical ideas include:

- A portion of Sunday, for example, from 9 AM until 2 PM

- Transition Saturday evening at 7 PM until Sunday at 2 PM (or return to regular residential schedule)

- Celebrating the entire weekend and creating a swap to avoid three weekends in a row.

BIRTHDAYS

First, let's discuss parents' birthdays:

- Is it important to me to see our children on my actual birthday?

- If so, does a two to three hour visit that doesn't disrupt their activities / studies work for me? Or, would I prefer that our children spend a night with me?

- If neither, are we comfortable knowing we'll celebrate our birthdays with the children during our individual residential time? (Celebrating birthdays is important to kids!)

- As co-parents, can we be sure to help our children make a call (or similar way to reach out) to their other parent on his / her birthday?

A child's birthday:

- Is it important to me to see our child on his/her actual birthday?

- If so, does a two to three hour visit that doesn't disrupt their activities / studies work for me? Or, would I prefer that our child spend a night with me?

- Consider how we'll define parent time with our child for his / her birthday when it falls on a week day, weekend day or if it should fall on a residential transition day.

Here are some examples of language to describe birthdays:

A. Child's Birthday: The child will reside with the parents according to the residential schedule. The non-residential parent has the option of a visit of up to two hours arranged by mutual agreement that does not disrupt dinner plans (unless agreed upon) or the child's regularly scheduled activities.

B. Parent's Birthday: The children will reside with the parents according to the residential schedule. The birthday parent has the option of a visit of up to two hours arranged by mutual agreement which may include dinner, but does not disrupt the children's regularly scheduled activities.

C. The child will reside with one parent (the mother) in even years and with the other parent (the father) in odd years. Birthday will be defined as (include times).

D. The child will reside with the parents according to the residential schedule. The residential parent will plan for the child's "family" dinner and invite the non-residential parent to attend with 14 days (designate lead time) notice. (Parents may agree that a neutral location for this event is best, i.e. a favorite restaurant, park, etc.)

Your Children's Peer Birthday Party:

You may have a birthday party for your child when you invite extended family / adult friends on your residential time, as might your co-parent. Kids love to be celebrated and to our knowledge, no child objects to multiple birthday cakes!

Sometimes children also have a birthday party for THEIR friends, their chums from school or the neighborhood. This is not typically an "adult" event, and is a strictly child-centered event. By agreeing to a peer birthday party, parents avoid any sense of competition about who gets to invite who to their children's parties.

Here are some things to consider when it comes to your children's peer birthday party:

- Who will project manage the birthday party? Will we rotate this responsibility every-other-year?

- Will we both be invited?

- Will we agree that it's best to have the party at a neutral location, or is it OK to have it at our homes?

- Will we limit other adults to those who we've agreed to invite? What about grandparents? Significant others?

- If one of us has a domestic partner / new spouse, will that person be included?

- How will we pay for the birthday party? Will the project manager be in charge of the budget and payment? Will we agree on a budget and split the costs? Will we set that budget now (establish an upper limit)?
- How much advance notice would we like from one another about the date and time of the party? 30 days?

Next, capture your agreements in writing.

EXAMPLE: "The parents will rotate the responsibility to project manage the child's peer birthday party: one parent (the mother) in odd years, the other parent (the father) in even years. The parents agree to a budget of up to $200 that will be split (how?). The parents will agree to a mutual date and time with at least 30 days planning notice. The party will be held at a neutral location. The party will be limited to children only unless otherwise agreed upon by both parents for the first two years post-divorce."

You can now include your unique decision points based on the questions above:

Celebrating our children's birthdays:

Managing our children's peer birthday parties:

Celebrating parents' birthdays

VIDEO III

TRANSITIONS, COMMUNICATION & DECISION-MAKING—

Other Important Factors in Your Parenting Plan

Insight & Inspiration:

Divorce Transition Can Be the Doorway to a Better You...

I challenge and encourage you to make your divorce not the event that defines you but the threshold that inspires you to do right by yourself and your children. To use this challenging transition as a catalyst and an opportunity to grow into a better person and a better parent by stretching in your maturity, communication skills, restraint, patience, understanding, and compassion. Seek to learn and grow rather than blame and resent; this is well worth the effort. You and your children benefit.

—**Lisa Gabardi**, Ph.D., author of *The Quick Guide to Co-Parenting After Divorce: Three Steps to Your Children's Healthy Adjustment*, is in private practice in Beaverton, Oregon, **www.gabardi.com** .

CHAPTER 12

Child-Centered Transitions— Smoothing the Wrinkles in Two-Home Family Life

Insight & Inspiration:

Put Your Feet in Your Children's Shoes....

There's a story about a little argument I had with my daughter over a hair straightener. She wanted to take it to her dad's one weekend, except, I wanted to use it as well.....needless to say, an argument ensued. And then it hit me. Why are we yelling over a hair straightener? I'm the adult, and the divorce was my choice. I want our kids to be comfortable in *both homes*. So, I bought one for her to always have.

This story might sound a bit trite. However, kids want to feel at home at both parents— and their needs and habits don't change from one home to the other. Having them pack-up all of their basics for every overnight becomes a constant reminder of the divorce. You can help. Provide your children with:

- Their preferred shampoo, conditioner, other hair products (especially important for teenagers), deodorant, underwear
- Girls— feminine hygiene (i.e. tampons, pads, etc), makeup if possible, hair accessories and brushes
- Boys—shaver, cologne and grooming accessories

Ask them what basics they need; go together to pick up the items; provide space in the medicine cabinet and shower *for their personal items*.

If you can, include them as you choose where you'll be living. Get them involved in picking their bedroom furniture, linens and so on. Ensure a place for their clothes, special items, and create a space for them to study. Being "at home" with a parent is important for kids...a little thoughtfulness can make a big difference.

—**Deborah Moskovitch** is a Divorce Coach, and bestselling author of *The Smart Divorce, The Smart Divorce Smart Guides and The Smart Divorce Audios*. **www.thesmartdivorce.com**

Child-Centered Transitions

Think of each transition from one parent's care to the other's as an emotional abyss your child must cross over. There is a moment, however brief, where your child must let go of connection and security with one of you and reach across to take the hand of emotional connection and security with the other. The more parents understand that transitions for children of all ages require mental, emotional and physical preparation followed by separation and reconnection, the better.

Help your children develop healthy rituals and practical approaches to packing their gear to move from one home to the other. Be supportive of the emotional reluctance and the all-too-often forgetting of something important. This can take time. Be patient. Your children will gain confidence and competence in time with their two-home transition process. Your job as the adult is to smooth out the wrinkles (the inconveniences) of living across two homes.

We often encourage that the current residential parent assist the children in preparing for the transition and then escort them to their other home where they will be joined by the other parent. This sends two important signals: 1) "I'm here to help you through this difficult transition," and 2) your other parent is not coming to "take you away from me" in a way that can be disconcerting for children.

Know that children physically transition in a matter of a couple of minutes, and will take another 30—60 minutes to transition emotionally. For the receiving parent, try and be present to your children as they arrive and begin the process of settling. Help them unpack, prepare a snack, take a few minutes on the couch to reconnect before setting demands when possible.

For young children who were dropped at school or daycare by one parent and are anticipating the pick-up of the other parent, the school or daycare time can be a bit more unsettled than on non-transition days. Consistency, ritual and some extra support from the teacher can help a little one as he / she establishes security in the rhythms of two-home family life.

Transitioning the Children's Belongings

Consider a clear plastic container with clip-on lid. Kids can decorate their "buckets" with stickers and plastic markers. You can help them secure a packing list in a plastic sleeve on the inside of the lid. The plastic containers fit easily in the car, keep things neat, and hold everything from basketball shoes to "My Little Pony" collections.

Remember: when children transition to and from school to their other home, you will have to transition their gear to their other home. By working together, you and your co-parent can make this as smooth and easy as possible.

Also, kids *will* want to move their things. Kids' belongings are theirs. They'll become attached to a particular hoodie or pair of jeans. Please don't mark their clothing or toys as if they belong to you or should be restricted to your home *regardless of who has purchased them*. These practices increase a child's feelings of being a "belonging"—someone who is fought over, whose belongings create conflict.

At the same time, all the pajamas can end up at one parent's home and the Lego's at another. Work with your co-parent to anticipate the need to rebalance clothing and toys at regular intervals. Remember: A parent's job is to smooth out the wrinkles of two-home family life for kids.

Insight & Inspiration:

Transitions are Tough; Love with Your Whole Heart....

Divorce is a significantly difficult time for the entire family. Emotions run high for parents *and* children.

My parents divorced when I was seven years old. My mother, sister and I moved to the United States from another country. So, I never had to go back and forth from one parent's house to the other like many children do of divorced parents.

Now as a step parent, I have learned that transition periods for a child can be challenging. It's important to have a room—at least a personal space—for your children at both homes. Help them feel "at home" with each of you.

Transitions are hard enough without having to take your daily necessities or all your things from one house to another. Consider doubling up on the basics, consider an extra pair of tennis shoes and plenty of casual clothes. Some things you can't avoid moving back and forth, like a favorite toy, school backpack or baseball equipment. Help your children by making that gear transition as easy as possible.

Once your children arrive, give them time to readjust, settle in and move through their own rituals of "coming home" to you. Understand and support your children if they want to call the other parent—even if they just left each other a few hours ago. The first day of transition can be a tough one. In time, with experience and rhythm, it will get easier and less emotional for everyone.

—**Angela Gleason** is a children's book author specializing in step-families and she resides in Cypress, Texas, **www.blendedbooks.com**

When Face-to-Face Transitions Don't Work

There are times, particularly when you and your co-parent are in the early stages of your family transition and emotions are high, that transitioning your children from one home to the other in person is too difficult. Don't despair! There are several options available that will help minimize conflict while still easing your children's transition between their homes.

Other options for successful transitions between co-parents include:

a)   Meeting at a mutually convenient neutral location, such as a fast food or shopping center parking lot;

b)   If heightened conflict exists, meeting at a mutually convenient location such as a police or fire station parking lot;

c)   Allowing for a neutral third party to provide transportation for the children between co-parents. Often times, a respected extended family member such as a grandparent or uncle, or a trusted adult friend, can be the temporary "go between." Just be sure the third party is neutral and is someone who is respected by both of you and not inclined to add drama to the situation. You also want to be sure this person has the best interests of the children at heart;

d)   Adjust the exchange times to coincide with when day care or school lets out, as long as the children know whom to expect for pick up or which bus to take.

"Kindness is for all times and in all situations—
not just when it suits us."

—Audrey Landrum

Transition Communication Checklist

Transition communication, whether provided by email or voicemail, are intended to help your co-parent be the best parent he/she can be to your child(ren). Consider what information is useful without managing the other household. Be constructive not instructive. If you don't have anything to communicate about many of the areas below, simply say, "School's good; friends are good" as a way of filling in the blanks.

School

☐ Homework follow-through / special project updates

☐ School to home communication that your co-parent may need

☐ Before / after school care updates

☐ Special events, concerts, awards, to share

☐ Extracurricular activity updates

☐ Special needs, tutoring, etc.

☐ Other

Friendships/Peer Relationships

☐ Anything to discuss about peer relationships—concerns or things to watch

☐ Updates on invitations, slumber parties, etc

☐ Social networking, phone use / texting, dating

☐ Other

Physical Health

☐ Updates on health-care appointments, rescheduled, etc.

☐ Other health care related issues—exercises, therapies, etc.

☐ Illness concerns—medications both prescribed or over-the-counter, fevers, rashes

☐ Physical complaints (tummy aches, headaches, etc)

☐ Changes in eating patterns

☐ Other

Emotional Well-Being

☐ Any mental health / anxiety-related concerns

☐ Sleep issues

☐ Difficulties with behavior

☐ Other

Discipline

☐ Self-management and self-organization

☐ Behavior programs and progress

☐ Other

Household Changes

☐ Changes in routines

☐ Other

Journal Moment 12

1. When I am the parent helping my children prepare for a transition to their other home, how can I best support a successful transition—both in terms of physically getting their belongings collected and moved, and emotionally working through the letting go of one parent...taking hold of the other parent?

_____

_____

_____

_____

_____

2. When I am the parent receiving our children as they make the transition from their other parent (or school or daycare), what will I do to help them create a sense of "arriving" and settling into their residential time with me—both physically (in terms of organizing their belongings), and emotionally (reconnecting)?

_____

_____

_____

_____

Transportation Arrangements

Areas for discussion:

- Our transition times are designated in our residential schedule—do we need to make any accommodation to those times based on the children's activity schedule or other intervening circumstance? (For example, rather than delivering the children at 4 PM as stated in the residential schedule, the receiving parent agrees to pick up the kids from swim lessons at the "Y" at 4:30.)

- How will we transition the children's gear? For weekend transitions? Week day transitions? To/from school, day-care? How about when school is not in session?

- What co-parenting guidelines will help us ensure healthy, neutral, cooperative transitions? What can we commit to?

- Location(s) for transfer(s)?

  - Each other's residence? Do we ever come into the other's foyer? Meet at the bottom of the stairs, or at the curb?

  - Do we prefer a neutral location midway between our two homes? A coffee shop, neighborhood park, or the parking lot of a police or fire station?

  - Do we need a third party to assist with calm, safe transitions?

  - Do we employ a service or person who provides a "safe zone" so we never transfer the children directly to one another, but rather through that person?

  - How will we handle unexpected schedule changes / delays / bad traffic?

- Who will be responsible for connecting the left-behind gear with the child who left it?

- Are there costs associated with transportation (airline tickets, bus or train fare) that need to be considered and addressed? If not here, will these be addressed in an order of child support or other such document?

You are now ready to bring together your transportation ideas. Here are examples:

A. The parent with whom the children are currently residing shall be responsible for transporting the children and their belongings to the receiving parent at the designated transition time.

B. The transitions will occur at school. The parent starting his / her residential time shall pick up the children from school and the other parent will deliver the children's belongings separately at an agreed upon time and location.

C. The parents will meet at the "coffee shop" located at (insert address) at the designated transition time and transfer the children and their gear.

Optional provisions for you to consider:

☐ **Unanticipated Delays:** The parents agree to provide each other a text message if possible when they are delayed by 15 minutes or more for transitions (*please do not text and drive*).

☐ **Conflict-Free Transitions:** Parents should work together to create smooth and safe residential transitions for the children. Parents will not use transition time to discuss adult information, sensitive issues or discipline. Parents will remember that transitions are stressful for the children. Parents will do what they can to ease their anxiety and increase stability. Brief, positive interchanges between co-parents are appropriate.

CHAPTER 13

Communication Protocols—
Sharing Information and Staying Connected

Insight & Inspiration:

"I'm just a Kid!"

Sometimes kids are asked to help a parent obtain information from or about another parent during a divorce. The requests may be made innocently enough and obviously without the intention of putting the children in the middle of their parents' divorce. However, they often do. Children should be able to know that they can love both parents without condition or restriction. Never feel they have to keep secrets or that they might be used as a private eye! Parents please understand your kids never need to be placed in the middle.

—**Matt Sossi**, Executive Director, Kids First Parents Second, is an attorney, writer and advocate for kids: **www.kidsfirstparentssecond.com**

Co-Parents' Communication Guidelines

H-E-A-R:

- **H**ealthy boundaries—respect privacy, be unobtrusive

- **E**ffective—desired outcome, constructive for your kids

- **A**greed upon—works for both of you

- **R**espectful—slow down, consider, manage emotions

When communicating by email or text:

- Communicate in your kids' best interest—remember, you are writing / speaking to your children's *other parent*, **not** your ex-spouse.

- Use a pleasant tone—speak or write with the very same tone to your BOSS.

- Make appropriate word choices—this is not the time for four-letter words or other expletives.

- Use **bold lettering** and ALL CAPS only for highlighting and ease of reading—**not** for shouting at the reader.

- Be brief, informative, well-organized—do your best to stay within the "200-word rule" for any one subject.

- Use the subject line of an email effectively / descriptively.

- Be thoughtful about how many communications you send—unless there is something urgent or time-sensitive, your transition email can be sufficient for healthy co-parent communication.

- Know that repetitive texts or emails are intrusive—please avoid badgering or harassing one another. This is unresolved spousal work.

- Respond in a timely manner to appropriate communications received, even if all you say is, "Got it. Will get back to you tomorrow," or whenever is appropriate and possible.

- Ignore unproductive emails, texts, or voice messages. Think of any response to negative / unproductive communication as kindling on a fire you're hoping will die-out. *Don't feed the fire.*

A quick review of the basics:

- Have you clearly stated the issue to resolve?

- Have you offered a potential solution?

- Have you stayed focused on your children and their needs?

- Have you maintained constructive civility?

- Have you asked yourself, "Is this communication actually necessary?" If not, delete.

Manage Emotions and Communicate Thoughtfully

Before any interaction (in person, phone, text, email) with your co-parent, pause and breathe. Meditate upon your love for your children and what they need from you. Remember your love for your children is greater than negative feelings toward your former partner. Then breathe some more and think about your highest values and the best version of you from which you want to act. Then breathe again and consider what to say or write.

—**Lisa Gabardi**, Ph.D., author of *The Quick Guide to Co-Parenting After Divorce: Three Steps to Your Children's Healthy Adjustment*, is in private practice in Beaverton, Oregon, **www.gabardi.com**

"The words you speak become the house you live in."

—Hafiz

Journal Moment 13

1. What is going to make the most sense in terms of how I stay connected when my children are not in residence with me?

a. You're always in their hearts, but not always on their minds. Do you want to risk interrupting or intruding on their world with the other parent by calling?

_____

_____

_____

b. Would you prefer to allow them to initiate calls and contact with you?

_____

_____

_____

c. Does it make sense to create predictable contact that is scheduled periodically, but doesn't negatively disrupt the flow of their activities / life with their other parent?

_____

_____

_____

2. What skills will I need to develop to be sure that my communication, both verbally and in writing, is respectful with my co-parent?

a. Breathe before sending?

_____

_____

_____

b. Check for B-I-F-F (Brief, Informative, Firm and Friendly)? (credit to Bill Eddy, for the development of the BIFF concept)

_____

_____

_____

Possible Communication Provisions

Please place a check in the boxes provided for those you'd like to consider including in your parenting plan.

☐ **Co-Parent Planning Meetings:** The parents shall have face to face meetings (or other agreeable method) in an agreeable location for up to two hours during the months of January, March, and August. In odd years, one parent (father) shall initiate the scheduling and the other parent (mother) shall initiate in even years. Parents may choose to cancel meetings by agreement. At these meetings, the parents will discuss the children's health care, developmental and educational needs, and other parenting issues as desired. Additionally, the following season-specific topics will be covered:

> **January meeting:** review the school schedule through the end of the school year, review school breaks and holidays and special occasions, and begin summer planning;

> **March meeting:** discuss the summer schedule, camps, activities, child care, summer vacations, and holidays;

> **August meeting:** review the upcoming school schedule from start of school through end of January to include winter break and holiday considerations.

Parents agree to use a co-parent coach (or other neutral facilitator) to assist with these meetings upon either parent's request. Parents agree to discuss how the cost of facilitation will be paid. These meetings, however, do not supersede the parents' responsibility to stay informed about the children's educational, health care, and extracurricular needs and schedules.

☐ **E-mail Communication:** The parents will rely on email to communicate pertinent information about the children and make joint decisions. The parents will place a clear message in the subject line, such as: "Request to change weekend drop-off time," "Joint decision needed on therapist," or "Dental appointment needed." Parents agree to the following email protocols:

☐ **Transition report:** The parents agree to provide each other a transition report within 12 hours of a transition to the other parent's home (frequency agreed upon) to facilitate healthy continuity between households and a sense of integration within the children's two-home family life.

☐ **Time sensitive email** will be identified in the subject line and the recipient will make every effort to respond as promptly as possible, and no later than within 24 hours. Parents agree to check email on a daily basis in order to respond to time-sensitive email.

☐ **Parents will respect each other's time** and will not send multiple emails on the same subject on a daily basis. When possible, parents shall collect communication topics and exchange emails once or twice weekly.

☐ **If a parent fails to respond** to a question or request within 48 hours, the initiating parent will contact the other by phone. If the requesting parent still receives no response or definitive answer within another 24 hours, she or he may move forward without further input.

☐ **Communication Access:** When the children are in residence with one parent, the other parent is allowed telephone, videoconference, or similar communication with the children at reasonable times and for a reasonable duration—and the children are allowed to contact their other parent in a similar fashion. In the event that a children's cell phone use is limited for disciplinary reasons, the parent will provide the children an alternative to facilitate communication with the non-residential parent.

☐ **Promoting Contact and Affection toward the Other Parent:** Each parent endeavors to promote the emotions of affection, love and respect between the children and the other parent.

☐ **Parent-Child Communication:** The parents will support and empower the children to discuss grievances or concerns directly with the appropriate parent. This might include role-playing with a child on how best to approach a subject or facilitating a meeting to allow the child to speak for himself / herself. Co-parents recognize the importance of listening to the children without instilling a fear of loss of love or criticism for raising concerns. Co-parents will honor the differences in parenting styles and household rules, and will instill in the children respect for both parents.

☐ **Negative Communications:** Both parents will protect the children from overhearing or participating in communications that blame, judge, or criticize the other parent. Each parent agrees to refrain from words or conduct that could estrange the children from the other parent, damage the children's opinion of the other parent, or impair the children's love and respect for the other parent. Each parent agrees to discourage others in the children's presence, including extended family and friends, from negative communication about the other parent.

☐ **Protecting the Children from Adult Matters:** Neither parent shall advise the children of the status of child support payments, payment for activities, or other legal matters regarding the co-parents' relationship.

☐ **The Children and Adult Information:** Neither parent shall use the children, directly or indirectly, to gather information about the other parent or take verbal messages to the other parent in a non-age-appropriate manner.

☐ **Travel Out of the Area for Overnights:** The parents agree to provide each other travel dates and times, means of transportation, and flight numbers (if relevant) when traveling with the children away from home and spending the night out of the area. Parents agree to provide the other with alternative contact information if cell coverage is limited or unavailable in the case of emergency.

CHAPTER 14

Decision Making—Parents as Co-Parent Executive Officers

Insight & Inspiration:

Two Things Kids Hate...

There are two things your children hate: your conflict, and the possibility that they are the cause of it. So any co-parenting plan that you *both agree to* is already a huge relief for them. Your ability to agree also creates a virtuous circle. If your children know you and their other parent can talk to each other and make decisions without war breaking out, they will have the confidence to raise any complaints or problems about the plan as it impacts on them. This gives you the vital information you need to modify things as time goes on. It also gives your children the reassurance that open dialogue is the route to positive change, not a one way ticket back to deadlock and division that they then have to feel responsible for.

—**Christopher Mills** is a psychotherapist, mediator, family-law consultant, and author of *The Complete Guide to Divorced Parenting*. Chris practices in the UK. **www.chrismills.uk.com**

Clear Communication is Key to Joint Decision Making

It is important to establish a plan between you and your co-parent regarding how you will make decisions for your children moving forward. There are three different types of decisions that parents typically face.

The first consists of those day-to-day decisions that tend to be made from common sense and are so minor they do not require input from a co-parent. These would include things such as whether your daughter can attend a slumber party during your residential time; whether your son can stay home sick from school when he has a fever; or dividing age-appropriate household chores between your children when they are with you.

The second type of decision making is emergency-related decision making in which there is simply no time to seek the input of the other parent. Examples include a medical emergency where a child needs to be rushed to the hospital, in the event of a weather or natural disaster, or a parent's own medical emergency.

The third type of decision making, which typically is expected to be jointly made, are those decisions that are non-emergency in nature but go beyond day-to-day decisions—having a significant impact on your children or a financial impact that is shared. These include non-emergency health care, such as elective surgeries, orthodontia, and counseling.

Other joint decisions can include decisions around religious upbringing including which place of worship to attend, as well as educational decisions including which school to attend (whether public, private, or home schooling), and day care providers. Other miscellaneous decisions often requiring joint participation can be found in the accompanying worksheet on decision making.

Co-parents with constructive communication make many of these decisions easily over a phone call and / or through email. We recommend that joint decisions that impact each parent's time or requires commitment on the other parent's residential time or a shared expense, be documented in email and shared. When decisions are non-urgent and are more developmental, they can be part of your agenda during your next co-parent business meeting.

If you need assistance in weighing the seriousness of a decision, or feel you require more information before making a decision, you might work together with the child's health care providers, teachers, etc. Lastly, you can always ask for help from a neutral facilitator to help you both discuss the implications and impacts of a decision you're struggling with.

Journal Moment 14

1. How did we make child-related decisions in the past with regard to:

A. Education?

_____

_____

_____

_____

_____

B. Healthcare?

_____

_____

_____

_____

C. Religion?

_____

_____

_____

D. Extra-curricular activities?

_____

_____

_____

2. How will I both "step-up" and "step-in" to become an effective Co-parent Executive Officer? Will I use business meetings? Email? What can I count on from my co-parent in terms of responsiveness and respect?

_____

_____

_____

_____

3. How will I remember, *before* I answer my child, that I will say, "Dad and I (or Mom and I) will talk about that and get back to you," when deciding whether our child can do something that changes the residential schedule and/or involves a financial commitment from my co-parent?

_____

_____

_____

_____

Decisions about Children

Day-to-day Decisions: Each parent will make day-to-day decisions in his / her own home. This includes: activities of daily living, discipline, household chores, basic healthcare needs, etc. Please be sure to inform your co-parent if and when you take your child for health care services in the case of illness.

Emergency Decisions: Each parent has the obligation to seek emergency healthcare for a child as needed.

Decision Type	By Whom?	Special Notes
MANDATORY ITEMS		
Educational Decisions • School choice, • Classes, school-related extended travel, etc. • College planning (college visits)		
Non-Emergency Medical Treatment (Choice of physicians / dentists, elective medical) • Routine health care • Non-routine healthcare • Changes in health care providers • Counseling / mental health		Current health care providers:
OPTIONAL ITEMS		
Extracurricular activities that impact both parents' residential time or require a shared expense		
Sex education courses		
Driver's education		
Acquiring a driver's license		
Car purchase by a minor child		
Car insurance (by whom/how paid for)		
Tattoos, body piercings, body alterations		
Child possessing his / her own cell phone		
Internet presence (e.g. Instagram, SnapChat, Facebook, Twitter, etc.)		

Screen time / devices (tablets, computer, TV, etc.)		
Marriage before age 18		
Military enlistment before age 18		
Before / after school care (day-care) provider		
Religious activities of children We have committed to raise our child in a particular faith:		
Child's passport		
International travel		
Gun use by a child		
Other:		
Other:		

Optional provisions for your consideration:

☐ **Inform:** The parents will develop a list of childcare providers/babysitters. Parents will share with one another the names, phone numbers and manner of acquaintance of babysitters / childcare providers.

☐ **Inform:** The residential parent will notify the non-residential parent as soon as reasonable in the case of extraordinary information regarding the children, including medical emergencies or visits to a health care provider, major school discipline, unusual or unexplained absence from the home or school, or contact with police or other legal authority.

☐ **Access to Professionals and Records:** Each parent shall have full and equal access to the educational, extracurricular activity, and health care records of the children. In addition, each parent shall have independent authority to confer with the children's school(s), therapists(s), healthcare providers and other programs or professionals with regard to the children's educational, emotional, physical, and social progress. As needed, both parents will actively assist and encourage care providers to provide the other parent access to the children's records and to confer with the other parent.

☐ **Participation in Religious Activities**: Each parent shall be entitled to have the children participate with them in their religious activities. Neither parent shall disparage the other parent's religious activities or attempt to sway the children to their respective religious or philosophical viewpoint.

CHAPTER 15

Paying for Children's Needs and Activities— Extraordinary Expenses, Kids and Money

Insight & Inspiration:

Raising Your Children "Together" Apart...

A co-parenting plan is going to be your guidebook to raising your children together. *Together* is the key word here.

No matter what happened between you and your ex, or what is happening now, it is time to move on and bury the relationship and the emotions that come along with it. It is vitally important to rise above and separate these emotions when building your co-parenting plan.

We have seen too many families ripped apart battling in court, the outcome is *never* good for anyone involved: the mother, the father and the kids all suffer, financially and emotionally.

The effects can be devastating.

Your agreed co-parenting plan can give you reassurance and peace of mind knowing what is expected of yourself and your ex, and how your children will be taken care of when away from their home with you. It is an enforceable guideline on how to raise your children, *together* apart.

Take this time to really dive deep and think about your children's needs first. As long as you are doing this in a collaborative approach that values the role of your ex as a parent in your children's lives, you should come away from this process inspired and empowered knowing your children will be well taken of, and that future conflicts will be minimized.

—**Renee Harrison** and **Jeremy Kossen** are co-parents dedicated to supporting parents through their separation / divorce process through DivorceBuddy: **www.divorcebuddy.co**

How Do Your Parenting Plan Provisions
and Financial Considerations Intertwine?

This is a question you should discuss with legal counsel in your jurisdiction. Typically, parenting plans and orders of child support are separate components to your overall legal action (whether separation, divorce, or a paternity action). An initial determination of child support is made based on both parents' incomes. Sometimes, however, once the child support determination is made, that child support can be adjusted based on different factors that may be allowed in your particular jurisdiction. Some of these factors may include expanded residential time for the parent obligated to pay support, special needs of the children, special tax considerations, or certain significant socioeconomic factors including significant wealth or financial hardship.

Many factors go into considering the child support obligation apart from the residential time a child may spend with the parent obligated to pay support. Therefore, it is important to seek legal advice whenever possible to make sure you and your co-parent understand your rights and obligations with respect to financial support of your children.

Other areas where your order of child support may interact with your parenting plan include:

- Payment for events, extra-curricular activities, and other extraordinary agreed expenses;
- How you implement decision making in situations where you share expenses and others where one parent covers expenses;
- How you pay for conflict resolution expenses;
- How you might share travel expenses in a parenting plan where extensive travel is involved as part of the residential schedule.

Get the information you need to make sound decisions.

When Parents Fight about Money

Children will need things from time to time. They'll come to you and ask if they can play an instrument in the band; they'll make the cheerleading squad. All of these activities and experiences cost money. Work with your co-parent to have a smooth protocol for making extra-curricular activity decisions in a timely manner, and pay for the necessary gear/expenses without confusion or conflict.

When parents fight over money that children request for their daily needs or their school extracurricular activities, they feel helpless and ashamed. Children know that two-home family life means that money may be tighter than it was before the separation / divorce. Talk frankly about what you can and can't afford without causing your children to feel bad for asking. Be that confident guide with sound money management and a good credit rating with your co-parent. As your children mature, guide them in earning their own money to contribute in responsible, age-appropriate ways.

Journal Moment 15

1. My co-parent and I will need a financial process for reconciling our agreed upon extraordinary expenses. (Extraordinary expenses are those expenses not covered by child support—expenses we agree to share.) How will the two of us keep a strong credit rating with each other as Co-Parent Financial Officers?

How will we:

a. Document our agreements for shared expenses?

b. Track and share receipts—will this be necessary?

c. Determine how often we settle / reconcile our expenses?

d. How will the money get transferred?

2. How will the two of us make sure that our children won't get caught in disagreements / conflicts about money?

_____

_____

_____

_____

_____

3. How and when will we include our children in paying their portion of certain expenses in a way that is age-appropriate and builds confidence?

_____

_____

_____

_____

4. What about "allowances"?

_____

_____

_____

_____

VIDEO IV
CHANGES, CONFLICT RESOLUTION, AND CO-PARENTING
Additional Guidelines for Completing Your Parenting Plan

Insight & Inspiration:

With Love Anything Is Possible...

*"Faith is taking the first step even when you
don't see the whole staircase"*
—Martin Luther King, Jr.

This quote reminds me of how important it was to take that first step towards healing even when my bed kept calling me to return to it. Divorce can stop you dead in your tracks. You become paralyzed by thoughts of the future and angry about stories from the past, all at the same time. It's like being in limbo. Trusting and believing in love is the first step to returning to the staircase of living...and to remembering that with love anything is possible.

—**Patricia Ann Russell**, is the author of, *The Divorce Ceremony, Healing Spirituality and Divorcing Amicably in Twelve Weeks,* as well as President, The Divorce Foundation and The Russell Consulting Group: **www.trcgconsulting.com**

CHAPTER 16

CHANGE—Short-term, Expected and Unexpected, and Long-term, Significant Change

Insight & Inspiration:

The Most Important Problems in Life We Must Outgrow...

Change can feel difficult. You're not alone if you find yourself saying, "I'd rather that things just stay the way they are (or the way they were), because at least the status quo is familiar, and I'm more comfortable with the familiar than I am with the unknown. I might be open to change, but only *if* I can be sure it will be change *for the better!*"

But this approach overlooks something very important: you don't know if change will be "good" or "bad" until *after* you've gone through it. And the final verdict on any given change may depend less on the circumstances than on what you bring to them—your attitude, your awareness, your approach. Carl Jung once wrote "the greatest and most important problems in life can never be solved, only outgrown."

As parents transitioning through divorce and into the next chapters of your life, the best thing you may be able to do—for your kids and for yourself—is to keep your focus on *out-growing* old beliefs and old behaviors, and on seeking what Jung called "a new and stronger life urge."

—**Dan Keusal**, M.S., LMFT is a Jungian psychotherapist in Seattle, and author of the acclaimed e-newsletter "Living with Purpose and Passion" available at **www.dankeusal.com**

Change is the One Thing You Can Be Sure Of

Whether you are in a two-parent household or are two-household parents, change is a fact of life. Your approach to change can make such a difference in your children's well-being, especially in two-household parenting. Take Arnie and Eva.

Arnie and Eva divorced five years ago. Over time, life changes led to a need to make changes to the existing parenting plan. The family home in the country where their two sons had grown up had been sold and everyone moved into a new neighborhood in the city where the boys were having all sorts of difficulties. They were struggling in school, with peers and in their neighborhood.

Arnie took a new job that required him to work four, ten-hour days leaving the boys unsupervised at his house during the week. Eva lost her job, creating financial stressors on both households. After four months of being out of work, Eva found an amazing job opportunity but it would require her to relocate about two hours from where the families were currently located.

They both agreed that her work would remove the financial pressures—the cost of living was lower in the area where she would be working. It was a more rural neighborhood and school, which would allow the boys to return to a more familiar lifestyle. While the boys had lived with Dad in a week on / off schedule, Dad never did do as well with structure, homework and emotional development as Mom did. Where he excelled was in spending time with the boys hiking, camping and fishing, and leading a Scout troop. He could do all those things with his three days off each week, allowing Mom to do the structure and routine while Dad was still involved with the boys.

Although it meant the boys relocated with their Mom, the connection between parents was strengthened and, in spite of the distance, the children continued to feel held, cared for and loved by both parents.

This is a shining example of where parents, in spite of old conflicts and fears, embraced the changes that life had presented. They adopted a stance of flexibility and adaptability which allowed them to use their imaginations to create the best possible outcome for their specific family at each specific point in time, setting an example for themselves and their sons for doing the same in the future.

—**Anne Lucas**, MA, LMHC is a therapist, Collaborative coach, teacher / trainer and mediator.
She is a co-founder of Seattle Collaborative Law Training. Anne has served as President of King
County Collaborative Law and Collaborative Professionals of Washington.
www.theevergreenclinic.com

When Travel Impacts Your Residential Schedule

Parents who travel for a living or have unusual work schedules often have an adjustment to make as they attempt to merge their travel schedule with the confines of a residential schedule. Most partners are used to their other parent at home providing back up when they travel—they come home and announce their travel schedule and the "at home" parent and the children make it work.

No more. You are committing to a residential schedule. Your former partner is no longer your automatic childcare backup for your travel dates. Although your co-parent may be willing to cover for you, most parents don't want their schedule dictated by their former spouse's work schedule. Do not assume you can expect him / her to cover for you and do be appreciative when he / she is willing to accommodate your travel schedule.

If you commit to a residential schedule, you now have new requirements to be home and on duty with your children in a way that you've not been restricted before. This can require crafting a residential schedule that allows for your travel; it can mean setting boundaries on your work (your boss?) about your availability. These are your responsibilities, not your co-parent's. Be realistic about residential schedule commitments—as much as you might want a 50 / 50 shared schedule, does your travel schedule allow you to be home to fulfill your obligations?

Scheduling travel on your child-free time and protecting your duty-parent days at home is a learning curve. Most parents struggle with the limitations / restrictions of a residential schedule until they get the hang of being both a duty parent and a responsive business owner or employee.

If your work involves constantly changing work schedules (physicians, pilots, military, fire fighters, etc), build in regular scheduling adjustments as part of the residential schedule in your parenting plan. You may need help to know exactly how to do this, but you can write in scheduling adjustments based on rotations or unpredictable work patterns that will meet both your co-parent's need for respect, and your need to have your work schedule accommodated so you can be an active and engaged parent.

When Should You Modify Your Parenting Plan?

A "major change" is when something occurs that makes it impractical to follow your residential schedule. The best example of a major change is relocation by either you or your co-parent to a location far enough away that the quality of the residential time is impacted by the length of time it takes to make the exchange.

Another example of a major change would be when one co-parent changes his or her work schedule to the extent that the children spend significant time with a third party caregiver rather than with one of the co-parents. Examples of this would be when one parent switches from day shift to night shift, or when one parent begins working weekends when they would have had residential time with their children.

When a major change occurs in either parent's life that causes the current residential schedule to be impractical, the following steps are often helpful with amending the parenting plan:

1) The parent who will be experiencing the change should give as much notice as possible to their co-parent prior to the change. The parent making the change should propose ideas to the other parent for how the residential schedule can be altered to remain functional.

2) Schedule a "business meeting" to discuss alternative schedules that will maximize the time the children spend with the parent requiring the change with the least amount of disruption, along with brainstorming options for transportation arrangements if the change results in long-distance travel.

3) Any agreements reached for amending the residential schedule should be put in writing. You should also seek legal advice as to whether a formal modified parenting plan needs to be filed with the court in your jurisdiction.

4) In the event you and your co-parent are unable to discuss the scheduling issues in an effective manner, utilize the services of a mediator or other neutral professional who can help you and your co-parent reach a durable agreement without having to go to court or having your children lose out on a relationship with either parent.

Journal Moment 16

1. What helps me prepare for change?

_____

_____

_____

_____

2. What helps our children prepare for and adapt to change?

_____

_____

_____

_____

Making Changes to Your Parenting Plan

During the lifespan of your parenting plan, you may experience short term and long term changes in your family life. Some will be expected and easy, and others may be unpredictable and require more significant adjustment. Here are some suggested ways to handle some of the typical changes in a two-home family's experience (optional provisions for you to consider):

☐ **Days Removed from School:** The parents agree that either of them may remove the children from school for up to (X number) days per academic year for the purpose of pleasure, travel, or to extend a vacation. Other days removed from school beyond these designated (X number) will require agreement.

☐ **Making One-Time Changes to the Schedule:** When parents make agreements to swap or trade time, they will confirm the changes in writing (email acceptable). The new agreement remains intact unless both parents mutually agree to reverse the adjustment of the schedule.

☐ **Schedule Adjustments:** Both parents recognize that circumstances are likely to change as the children mature, and the residential schedule may need to be adjusted to accommodate those changes. By mutual agreement, the parents may make revisions in writing to the residential schedule to address the children's schedule changes, activities, and other changes in circumstances. Neither parent is required to agree to any proposed revisions of this parenting plan. Such adjustments shall be effective at the time they are agreed to in writing and acknowledged by both parents (written agreements and acknowledgement by email is acceptable). If no agreement is reached, the parents may work toward a resolution using their chosen conflict resolution process.

☐ **Substantial Work Schedule Change:** If a parent's work schedule substantially changes, thereby impacting his or her capacity to meet ongoing residential time with the children, the parents will work together to modify the schedule to meet the needs of the children to maintain an engaged and secure relationship with each parent. Once agreed upon in writing, the parents may seek legal advice on next steps, which could include filing an updated parenting plan with the courts.

☐ **Current Residential Information:** The parents will provide each other with the address and telephone number of their residences and update such information promptly when it changes.

☐ **Relocation:** In the event that a parent is relocating from the area and this change of residence directly impacts the children's school attendance or the residential schedule, the parents will work together to modify the schedule to meet the needs of the children for a predictable and functional residential schedule with each parent. Once agreed upon in writing, the parents may seek legal advice on next steps, which could include filing an updated parenting plan with the courts. If no agreement is reached, the parents may work toward a resolution using their chosen conflict resolution process.

☐ **Modify a Provision of this Plan:** In the event that either parent wishes to review and modify a provision of this parenting plan, then he or she will send a written request to the other parent, and the parents will work together to address the question and any related issues. Except in case of an emergency that endangers the health or welfare of a child, if the parents are unable to reach a mutual agreement on their own, the parents will use their chosen conflict resolution process identified in this parenting plan prior to court involvement.

CHAPTER 17

Conflict Resolution— Setting Priorities, Solving Problems

Insight & Inspiration:

Mindful Self-Care for You and Your Children...

Learning how to manage your emotions and emotional reactivity might be the single best skill you can develop to be an effective co-parent. Pause and breathe slowly before you react. Become aware of your triggers and observe your feelings. These steps will slow the fight-flight reaction and help you engage your thinking and planning brain. Once you can access your thinking brain you can consider your children, your values, and your goals. Emotion regulation is an empowering skill! Need help managing your emotions? Reach out to a counselor or coach—now's the time to invest in a better future for you and your kids.

—**Lisa Gabardi**, Ph.D., author of *The Quick Guide to Co-Parenting After Divorce: Three Steps to Your Children's Healthy Adjustment*, is in private practice in Beaverton, Oregon, **www.gabardi.com**

Establishing Priorities in the Residential Schedule

Your parenting plan includes designations for 365 days a year, 24 hours each day. You have discussed daily schedules, summer schedules, and vacation with parents, school breaks, holidays, and special occasions. You'll discover there is opportunity for conflict that results from designating particular types of time with each parent when those different types of time can actually overlap! One way to "break the tie" if you will, is to actually agree on ranking the importance for the various types of time.

One example could look like this:

1. Special occasions
2. Holidays
3. School breaks
4. Vacation with parents
5. Daily schedule (summer or school)

Now you would know that if a child's birthday fell on the same day as a holiday, and if one parent was designated for residential time for the holiday and the other parent was designated time for the child's birthday, that parent designated for the birthday (a special occasion) would "win" the time conflict. Let's look at another prioritization:

1. Vacation with parents
2. School breaks
3. Holidays
4. Special occasions
5. Daily schedule (summer or school)

This list of priorities tells us that these co-parents value travel. They've placed their vacation choice at the very top—a parent's vacation with children could take priority over a holiday or special occasion. They've listed school breaks in second priority as they see those breaks as additional opportunities for travel. These parents believe they can celebrate holidays and special occasions at alternate times as needed or while they're traveling.

You can see that setting priorities reflects values, traditions, and preferences. Working together to rank the importance of the various types of time will help you when those occasional conflicts emerge over the types of time.

The Importance of a
Conflict Resolution Provision

Despite your best efforts, there may be times when you and your co-parent are simply unable to reach an agreement on your own about something that is very important to one or both of you. Rather than allowing a disagreement to escalate into conflict that may negatively impact your relationship with each other, or worse, negatively impact your children, it is wise to seek assistance from a trained professional who can help facilitate difficult conversations. The use of a mediator or a counselor or family therapist trained in mediation skills can go a long way toward reducing the conflict, and help you both break apart the components of the issue to manageable levels.

A good mediator will help you and your co-parent determine whether your disagreements are based in facts, value judgments, or emotions and will help you understand one another's perspectives. Often times just feeling heard by someone else, along with being able to weigh the pros and cons, strengths and weaknesses of various options, you and your co-parent will be able to reach compromises in areas where you may have thought agreement was impossible.

Most jurisdictions require a conflict resolution provision within the parenting plan to encourage co-parents to seek outside assistance *first* before clogging up the overextended court system with issues that can be resolved with neutral professionals trained to utilize a problem-solving approach. In situations where the mediator is unable to assist with resolving the conflict or dispute, using the expertise of family-centered attorneys for the legal standing of the issue can be another useful step.

In severe situations, parents may want the judge's rule to prevail and settle their conflict, or parents may believe going to the court is the only way to ensure adequate protection for their children. In these situations, the courts are available and ready to protect children and their interests.

Healthy Conflict is Inevitable;
Toxic Conflict is Traumatic for Kids

Almost all parents claim that their children mean more to them than anything else in the world. Inadvertently, many of those same parents cause their children trauma. High levels of parental conflict can cause childhood trauma. In marriage or divorce, it is the chronic and/or toxic parental conflicts that are extremely harmful to children—not divorce *itself*.

A great deal has been written about the fact that when spouses feel compelled to win their arguments with each other, they end up losing their relationship. If the need to win arguments was destructive to the marriage, then fighting to prove a point or win an argument as co-parents is going to be even less well-received.

Conflict is a fact of life and occurs for a variety of reasons, such as differing perspectives, priorities, or solutions to a problem. For example, there are different ways to parent kids. Parenting styles are a matter of perception. Children benefit from your differences as much as they benefit from your similarities. Unless your parenting differences are endangering your child, then don't allow those differences to become a source of chronic/toxic conflict. Because we know for sure that chronic/toxic conflict is distressing—and often traumatic—for kids.

Healthy conflict is inevitable and, when handled skillfully, is growth-producing for kids. Children need parents who are bigger than their problems. Children benefit when co-parents resolve conflict and model mature problem-solving. The end goal is to be better parents to your children and manage conflict constructively.

—**Mark B. Baer** is a mediator and attorney, who has been practicing in Los Angeles for almost 25 years, with an office in Pasadena, California.
www.markbaeresq.com

Journal Moment 17

1. How do I want to prioritize the various kinds of time? Do I want to prevent a summer vacation in order to see my child on his or her summer birthday?

_____

_____

_____

_____

2. Who do I recommend we work with if we run into conflict and need help from a mediator or facilitator?

_____

_____

_____

_____

Priorities under the Residential Schedule

Please consult with your legal counsel on how priorities are established in your jurisdiction. Consider the following types of time designated in the residential schedule. Work with your co-parent to prioritize which types of time are most important to the two of you as you plan for and co-parent your children:

- Daily schedule (summer or school)
- Vacation with parent
- School breaks
- Holidays
- Special occasions

List the above in order of importance if / when a conflict should happen you will know which will prevail:

1. _____

2. _____

3. _____

4. _____

5. _____

Conflict Resolution

(The court-mandated form in your jurisdiction will provide structure and specific language for your conflict/dispute resolution process. The following is for consideration and assistance in terms of understanding the purpose and value of the conflict resolution provision of a parenting plan. This is language specific to the process recognized in Washington state, USA. Please consult with your legal counsel on the best provision for your jurisdiction.)

The parents have used the following principles in forming their agreement. Although these principles are not in themselves intended to be enforceable in court, the parents agree to do their utmost to uphold these principles in carrying out this parenting plan and their dispute resolution process:

Co-Parenting Guiding Principles *(You could insert Co-Parenting Guiding Principles from your Parenting Plan Worksheet from Chapter 4)*

Dispute Resolution Principles:

In the event of disputes, the parents agree to be guided by the foundational principles they adopted in reaching their agreements:

☐ Acting with honesty, transparency, and candor;

☐ Demonstrating cooperation, respect, integrity and dignity;

☐ Identifying and addressing the interests and needs of all;

☐ Focusing on the well-being of the children and themselves;

☐ Committing to resolving matters directly and without court intervention.

In applying these principles, the parents agree to consider the following:

1. Are we putting our children's needs and interests ahead of any negative feelings toward each other?
2. Are we maintaining the integrity of a strong and accessible parental relationship with both parents?
3. How are we conveying an atmosphere of respect and positive regard for each other?

The parents will use the following process for resolving future disputes relating to any parenting matter:

Prior to initiating the formal conflict resolution process, the parents have the option of making a bona fide effort to resolve their dispute directly, guided by the principles above. If expert input appears beneficial, the parents may want to seek advice from their attorneys on how best to include appropriate professionals in a neutral and safe way—gathering information to be used in reaching agreement.

In the event the above process is insufficient to bring resolution of the conflict, the parent who wishes to initiate the formal dispute resolution process will send (in written form—letter or email) to the other parent stating something such as, "I am initiating the dispute resolution process in Section V of the parenting plan regarding (followed by a description of the issue)." The receiving parent will respond within 72 hours with his / her intention to either resolve the dispute immediately in a mutually agreeable fashion or participate in scheduling an appointment with the appropriate third party.

The parents have agreed on the following progression of dispute resolution:

1. Meet with a divorce coach, child specialist or mediator, depending on the issue;
2. Consult family-centered attorneys in an attempt to resolve the issue;
3. Use their legal counsel to determine whether arbitration or court intervention is appropriate.

(The parents will include in their conflict resolution provision how the fees for these services will be paid.)

Any mediator or arbitrator will have the authority to order one party to pay a majority of all the fees incurred in conflict resolution if that party appears to be acting in bad faith.

In the conflict resolution process:

a) Preference shall be given to carrying out this parenting plan.
b) Unless an emergency exists, the parents will use the designated process to resolve disputes relating to implementation of the Plan, except those related to financial support.
c) A written record shall be prepared of any agreement reached at any step in the conflict resolution process and provided to each parent.
d) If the Court finds that a parent has used or frustrated the conflict resolution process without good reason, the court shall award attorney's fees and financial sanctions to the other parent.
e) The parents have the right of review from the conflict resolution process to the Superior Court.

"No tree has branches foolish enough to argue amongst themselves."

—Native American Wisdom

CHAPTER 18

Co-Parenting Guidelines— Successful Co-Parenting for Your Children's Future

Insight & Inspiration:

Turning Mistakes into a Wonderful Opportunity for Growth...

Mistakes are only harmful if you don't care about making them. If you do care, what happens next can be a wonderful opportunity for healing and growth. So when you bad-mouth your children's other parent in front of them (and you'll be superhuman if you never do that), just quietly follow up with, "I'm sorry sweetheart, I shouldn't have said that. I know you hate it when I talk about Mom / Dad like that, and I completely understand why." This instantly gives three reassuring messages. One, occasional expression of angry feelings is normal, you can recover, and doesn't have to lead to a flood of guilt or self-recrimination; two, whatever your personal feelings, you honor and support the vital role their other parent has in your children's lives; three, you respect your children's feelings as being separate from your own and don't require them to 'suck up' your suffering too...just because you're having to.

—**Christopher Mills** is a psychotherapist, mediator, family-law consultant, and author of *The Complete Guide to Divorced Parenting*. Chris practices in the UK. **www.chrismills.uk.com**

Other Provisions to Include in Your Parenting Plan

We have included in your worksheets a section called "Other Provisions." Although many of these provisions are not included as boilerplate choices in pattern parenting plan forms provided by different jurisdictions, many of these provisions can be added as an addendum page. Review carefully the various options and determine whether or not you and your co-parent wish to include any of them as co-parenting guidelines or agreements to enhance your children's two-home family life.

Whether or not you choose to actually incorporate any of the suggested terms into your parenting plan, discussing them with your co-parent is valuable. That will give you an idea in advance where potential problems may lie for the future. Not everything can be resolved in advance, but we know that attempting to determine where you and your co-parent may have similar beliefs, and where you may have disparate beliefs, can help you understand how to work with one another's parenting styles as you move forward, keeping your children's best interest at heart.

Building a "Blended Family Plan"

Getting from ex-partners to 'colleague-parents' is hard enough. And then, when you're finally getting the hang of it…. a new love comes into your life. Great, of course! However, it requires readjusting once more.

How to incorporate your new partner into your life and that of your children? How will your children accept this new adult into their family? And what if your new partner has children—how will they react? And last but not least, how will this influence the hard-won balance with your co-parent and the Parenting Plan you agreed upon? An experiment at best: statistics show a 60% breakup among blended families in the first year.

Or vice versa: your co-parent is re-coupling. You're being asked to relook at agreements, accept someone who may feel like an interloper in your children's lives, or change routines to fit for everyone involved. How to handle that?

Forging a blended family requires thoughtful planning and skill. Building a *Blended Family Plan* will help everyone adjust to the new situation. Together we look at boundaries, new roles, parenting styles, authority, decision-making, finances and many other subjects and aspects you may never have anticipated.

The education, understanding and respectful boundaries created through the development process help the adult relationships get off on the right foot. The plan creates clarity and helps to make the necessary transition for co-parents, step-parents and children manageable. Here's your chance to even the odds in this challenge—and maintain that all-important stability for kids!

*—**Kitty Duell** is a renowned international mediator, trainer and lecturer. She is an expert trainer in the field of International Family Mediation, Blended Family Plans, Mediation in Criminal Law, and Online Mediation. www.mediationkit.com*

111

Journal Moment 18

1. What are my concerns and worries about entering into a parenting plan agreement with my co-parent?

2. How can I best mitigate my concerns and build the best platform for successful co-parenting possible?

3. Can I talk with my co-parent and use the "Other Provisions" or information from "The Co-Parents' Handbook" to guide conversations about how the two of us will do things?

Possible Co-Parenting Guidelines

The following guidelines are intended as co-parenting guidelines only, and may or may not be enforceable in any court. The parents have chosen to include these as best practices for their future co-parenting relationship and will consult with their lawyers on enforceability:

☐ **Good Faith:** Both parents freely commit themselves to this parenting plan with the expectation that together they will provide a stable two-home life for the children. Both parents agree that unnecessary conflict, instability, unpredictability, and bad faith use of the conflict resolution provisions are harmful to children and will be avoided. Each parent will endeavor to promote the emotions of affection, love and respect between the children and the other parent.

☐ **Honoring the Residential Schedule:** Neither parent will encourage the children to change the residential schedule through any form of resistance (including refusal to transition at the appointed time) or lead the children to believe that they may choose their residential schedule. Changes to the residential schedule will be made by the co-parents or, absent agreement, through the conflict resolution process or the court system.

☐ **Corporeal Punishment:** Both parents agree that the children will be protected from any individual who would use physical or corporeal punishment as a means of discipline.

☐ **Gun Possession:** Each parent will **inform** the other in the event that he or she maintains a gun in his or her residence. Both parents commit to following the "best practices" for gun safety in the home, including keeping guns in locked cases with ammunition stored separately.

☐ **Best Safety Practices and Guidelines:** The parents agree to utilize the safety practices and guidelines established by the authorities in your jurisdiction (i.e. American Academy of Pediatrics and similar agencies) in making decisions and in resolving disputes, e.g. utilizing car seats or age-appropriate progression of entertainment content, etc.

☐ **Children Attending Their Activities:** Each parent has the responsibility to ensure that the children attend school and other scheduled activities while in that parent's care. Activities that affect both parents' residential schedules require co-parent agreement before involving or informing the children. Activity costs will be shared by the parents as outlined in the order of child support. Each parent shall have the authority to determine when a child should miss a scheduled activity for reasons of health and well-being.

☐ **Parental Involvement in School and Extracurricular Activities:** Both parents may participate in school and extracurricular activities for the children regardless of the residential schedule.

☐ **Current Residential Parent in Charge at Public Events:** When both parents are attending public events, the residential parent is in charge of the children. The non-residential parent shall defer to the other parent for routine decision making. The non-residential parent shall work to ensure that contact with the children does not unreasonably interfere with the normal flow of the activity or undermine the residential parent's authority.

☐ **Financial Obligation:** Neither parent shall financially obligate the other parent regarding the children without the consent of the other parent, unless otherwise provided in the order of child support.

☐ **Shared Family E-Calendar:** The parents agree to use a shared e-calendar to track the children's appointments, activities and schedules. The parents will update the calendar regularly and work together to make it an effective and useful tool.

☐ **Text Communication:** The parents agree that text messages typically are most useful for short and time-sensitive informational exchanges between them. Any significant co-parent communication or discussion will not occur via texting, but rather verified in email or writing.

☐ **Non-Parental Childcare Options:** Co-parenting works best when parents are thoughtful with each other in offering additional time with the children. When one parent has a conflict with his or her scheduled residential time, she or he may offer the time to the other parent. Some parents may choose to trade residential time to accommodate conflicting plans, and the parents acknowledge that children typically benefit by spending time with parents rather than child-care providers. However, the parents acknowledge that the children also benefits from expanded relationships and a variety of child-care options, so the parents will work together to enable the children to enjoy time with extended family of both parents, occasional babysitters, and participate in sleepovers with peers.

☐ **Screen Time:** Parents agree that the residential parent will provide appropriate limit-setting and monitoring of the use of electronics and screen-based communication devices in a healthy, respectful, and socially appropriate manner.

☐ **Child's Personal Items:** The parents agree that the children may move their personal items (e.g. clothing, portable electronic devices, cell phones, comfort items, meaningful possessions) between households. Parents agree to return any items at the children's residential transition time or upon request.

☐ **Parental Responsibility to Stay Informed:** Parents will stay apprised of the child's athletic, school, social and extracurricular events. The parents both shall make arrangements with the child's schools to obtain copies of school newsletters, report cards, and any other written materials. If the information can only be obtained or received by one parent, the parent receiving the information shall provide it to the other parent in a timely manner.

☐ **New Romantic Relationships:** Parents agree to inform one another prior to introducing the children to a new romantic partner, so that both parents can support the children in normalizing adult relationships.

☐ **Step-Parenting Considerations:** If and when a new step-parent enters the children's lives, the co-parents will consider a step-parent/blended family plan to facilitate the smooth integration of the adult with the children and diminish conflict between households. They will use a co-parent coach as needed for this process.

CHAPTER 19

Co-Parenting Alone—What if Your Co-Parent *Won't* Co-Parent?

Margy's Story

I was 19 when I met my first husband, Bob. We were married two years later.

I was thrilled when I discovered I was pregnant! Bob worked a lot and I went to his workplace to share the news. During the pregnancy he would say that he wanted me to have the baby on a Saturday night, rest up on Sunday, and then he could go back to work on Monday. I thought he was kidding.

I thought wrong.

I accommodated Bob's schedule and went into labor on a Saturday evening. Our daughter, Sharon, was born only six hours later. Bob went home and returned to the hospital on Sunday for a visit. On Monday morning, he picked us up, dropped us at home, and went back to work.

I became isolated and lonely. Bob really was not kidding about his job being a priority. He thought the rest of life should go on just fine. I was alone most days and nights, learning to be a mother, and dealing with a baby who didn't sleep. I thought fatherhood would change Bob—he would engage more. I also thought if I just loved him enough, was sexy enough, was a great housekeeper and cook, he would put the job aside, at least during the weekends.

Wrong again.

I started therapy. I wanted to learn how to deal with the loneliness and/or how to get Bob to be my companion. I'll never forget when my therapist said, "Some people are just not capable of this type of companionship or connection." He helped me realize: this wasn't about me. This was who Bob was, and I could not change him.

We separated when our daughter was eleven months old. Bob was not a co-parent from the beginning, except for financially, and even that became problematic. He was angry about the divorce and resented sending me money for child support. I learned early on that I couldn't rely on him for anything.

Although Bob's priority was his work, Sharon loved her daddy and I did need to let her see him. However, I had to call to ask him to come and see her. Bob would make promises he wouldn't keep and I learned quickly to stop telling Sharon that "Daddy was coming." Bob would either not show at all, or be hours later than promised.

It was so sad to see her standing at the window watching for him. If he finally appeared, she would squeal with excitement! He would come in and *shake her hand*.....no hugs.....he didn't pick her up. In all this pain, I often secretly wished for Sharon to not have to know Bob—to be free of his cold detachment.

Then there were the occasional times he would want her to go to his house, or go to his parents' house with him. Although Bob's parents were always very good to Sharon, we did not share the same values when it came to raising children. They displayed Sharon like a trophy, showing her off to their friends, never seeing her for who she was.

During those times, I had to let go of so much. I was powerless over what she ate, what TV shows she was exposed to, what movies they watched, who was around her, and how they spent their time with her. Bob's parents just laughed at me when I made suggestions for healthy food choices or activities for Sharon. I always shared with them what her schedule was and what her likes and dislikes were, although they didn't pay attention to my requests. I knew my daughter like no one else, and I felt I needed to protect her, or to at least do what I could to make her visits with Bob and his family easier for her.

When Sharon was 17 months old, she contracted H-flu meningitis. Again, I thought maybe this would jolt Bob into appreciating her. Wrong again.

I called Bob and he said he was busy working. I had just met Dave, whom I would eventually marry, and when I called him, he came right over, helping me with attempts to lower Sharon's temperature. I finally rushed Sharon to Children's Hospital; she began having grand mal seizures as soon as we arrived. She then went into a coma for the next ten days. The doctors said they didn't know if she was going to live. My family members and I stayed at her bedside, praying, singing, and visioning her in perfect health.

Miraculously, Sharon awoke and her healing began. Bob finally came to the hospital on Day 13, the day before she was discharged.

From the beginning, Sharon was very fond of Dave and began calling him "Daddy" after hearing his three-year-old son calling him "Daddy." However, one morning after we began living together, Sharon, who was then two years old, turned her cheek to Dave, snubbing him as he said good bye for the day. When I asked her about it after he left, she said, "I love my daddy-Bob." So I reassured her that she had two daddys who loved her, and she was a lucky girl. She thought about this for a short moment and, with a big smile, replied, "OK Mama." From that moment, there was never an issue with torn loyalties for her.

When Sharon was five, we moved from California to Oregon for Dave's work. In a way, I was relieved that Sharon would no longer be disappointed by failed visits from Bob. The down side was that I had to put her on an airplane to visit Bob and his family about twice a year. Talk about letting go! I hated having to do this.

Sharon was always excited to go and loved flying. However, she seemed to get sick during these visits, sometimes seriously sick. I always surmised this was due to the stress she felt by it all. I remember that she would cling to me for days after returning home.

The years went on and though Sharon had her "other" family in California, Dave and I were her grounding force. Bob chose not to be involved with decisions about her life. All of Sharon's activities, choices, successes and bumps in the road were shared by Dave, our extended families, and me. Sharon continued to visit her California family, but as she got older, she became more vocal about not wanting to go. Eventually the visits dwindled.

I have certainly come to accept that there is nothing I could have done to change Bob and his inability to connect with us, no matter what I tried to do to make myself more attractive or "better" in his eyes. My prayer is that Sharon has come to realize this as well. I have always known that having a biological father who was disconnected was part of her journey and that she would need to make sense of it one day for herself.

I have always felt powerless in this part of her life. What Sharon and I have done is to be open about the lack of connection, and jointly sort of marvel at and feel baffled by Bob's distance from us. In the meantime, Dave continues to be "the dad," a steady presence in her life. I will be forever grateful to Dave for how he has always loved her and connected with her like his own child.

Sharon is now married with two children of her own. At her wedding, both Dave and Bob walked her down to the middle of the aisle, where I was waiting for her. I then walked her the rest of the way. This only seemed fitting and right.

Bob only recently met his grandchildren for the first time. So, as the journey continues as these beautiful grandchildren are born and growing, I find the Serenity Prayer to be so true and helpful.

God, grant me the serenity to accept the things I cannot change,

The courage to change the things I can,

And the wisdom to know the difference.

—**Margy Clair**, MC, LMHC is a Life Coach and licensed mental health counselor with over 25 years experience partnering with those who want to create a life of their choosing. She walks her talk and feels honored to be invited into her clients' lives as a coach, cheerleader, and catalyst for change. Margy has been married to the love of her life for almost 33 years. She is the mama of two, mama-in-law of two, and nana of four.
www.covisionwellness.com

Journal Moment 19

1. If I am likely to be co-parenting "alone," my commitments to myself to provide the best role-modeling I can for my children, and to facilitate what I can for a healthy, well-supported childhood, are as follows:

_____

_____

_____

_____

2. How will my own faith and trust support me as I walk forward: what will I rely on to give me strength? Who will be *there* for me? Where can I turn in times of need?

_____

_____

_____

_____

_____

_____

_____

Insight & Inspiration:

As Haddaway asks, "What is Love?"

When my parents divorced at the end of my senior year, it forced me to reconsider what love and commitment means. It was a reminder that, though my parents are incredible people, they were not and are not perfect. One of the greatest gifts they gave me during an otherwise challenging time was humility—both of them explained, without anger toward the other, how they played a role in the divorce. They took ownership without giving blame. They were honest, with me and with themselves, about their mistakes and imperfections. Most importantly, they were committed to practicing forgiveness towards each other and vocal in their commitment to always practice loving me to the best of their ability.

Divorce is a challenging time in so many ways, but one often forgotten side effect is how it challenges young people's idyllic idea of love. As parents, one of the best gifts you can give is to help them understand that love is not always perfect, but even in the messiness and mistakes, love can be shown through humility, honesty, forgiveness, kindness, and commitment. That one of the most important kinds of love is the love we choose to practice even when it is uncomfortable or challenging or inconvenient.

—**Houston Kraft** is a keynote speaker, leadership trainer, and kindness advocate who specializes in working with middle school through college-age students: **www.houstonkraft.com**

ADDENDA

ON-LINE RESOURCES FOR
RESIDENTIAL SCHEDULE PATTERNS

The American Academy of Matrimonial Lawyers provides a free booklet that includes many residential schedule options: **http://aaml.org/ccrg**

Custody XChange provides a variety of schedules to consider: **http://www.custodyxchange.com/examples/schedules/**

ON-LINE CO-PARENTING AND PARENTING
PLANNING RESOURCES AND PUBLICATIONS

Shared Parenting Works provides parenting planning and co-parenting information: **http://sharedparentingworks.org/free-parenting-plans/**

"A Guide for Shared Parenting and Joint Custody" by Association of Family and Conciliatory Courts: **https://www.afccnet.org/resource-center/resources-for-families/pamphlet-information/categoryid/1/productid/3**

Help Guide—a non-profit guide to mental health and well-being: **http://www.helpguide.org/articles/family-divorce/co-parenting-tips-for-divorced-parents.htm**

CONTRIBUTORS

With much gratitude, we appreciate the following contributors to
"The Parenting Plan Handbook"

Mark B. Baer, Esq. is a mediator and family law attorney in Los Angeles, California. He has received much recognition both as a mediator and attorney and was most recently recognized as "Most Compassionate Family Mediator—California" in *Corporate America Legal Elite* of 2015. His article, "The Perfect Storm: Lawyer Limitation and the Adversarial Model in Family Law," published in the *American Journal of Family Law*, Winter 2014, is utilized at the Strauss Institute for Dispute Resolution at Pepperdine School of Law. **www.markbaeresq.com**

C.Joybell.C is an author of philosophy of mind, poetry, fiction, and other things wise and wonderful. She has been quoted by global leader and entrepreneurial innovations giant, Mosongo Moukwa; powerhouse entrepreneur, speaker and author, Guy Kawasaki; Dr. Dale Archer, *NY Times* bestselling author, founder/CEO of The Institute for Neuropsychiatry; Chanel Supermodel Cara Delevingne; Demi Lovato; Amanda Seyfried; and many, many more. She is also member of the Editorial Board of the *Polish Scientific Journal*, "Studia Humanitatis Mrongoviensis." **www.cjoybellc.com**

Margy Clair MC, LMHC is a Life Coach and licensed mental health counselor. She is the author of *The 5 Steps to Forgiveness*, and she practices in Gig Harbor, Washington. **www.covisionwellness.com**

Karen Covey is a divorce attorney, advisor, and author of *When Happily Ever After Ends: How to Survive Your Divorce Emotionally, Financially and Legally*. She practices in Chicago. **www.karencovy.com**.

Gary Direnfeld, MSW, RSW is a social worker, media personality, author, parenting columnist and speaker. Courts in Ontario, Canada consider him an expert in social work, marital and family therapy, child development, parent-child relations, and custody and access matters. **www.yoursocialworker.com**

Kitty Duell is a renowned international mediator, trainer and lecturer. She is an expert trainer in the field of International Family Mediation, Blended Family Plans, Mediation in Criminal Law, and Online Mediation. **www.mediationkit.com**

Tara Eisenhard is a child of divorce as well as an ex-wife and previous partner of a divorced dad. From these life experiences came her beliefs that a marriage shouldn't survive at the expense of its participants, and families should evolve, not dissolve, through the separation process. She is the author of the book *The D-Word: Divorce Through a Child's Eyes* and the blog *Relative Evolutions*. Her material has also been featured by Family Affaires, Divorcedmoms.com, *The Huffington Post*, and *Step Mom Magazine*. **www.taraeisenhard.com**

Carolyn Flower is a PR, Promotion & Brand Architect. As a *champion of change* entrepreneur, she mentors others to begin within, inspiring them to "refocus the lens" in various areas of their lives, discovering the "art of their possible." She is a passionate first person advocate for the collaborative divorce philosophy, and author of *Gravitate 2 Gratitude—Journal Your Journey*. Her second book, *Family Ever After (Collaborate Life after Divorce—Embrace a New Normal)*, is forthcoming in 2016. Carolyn is a blog contributor at *The Huffington Post* (Divorce). **www.carolynflower.com**

Lisa Gabardi, Ph.D. is a licensed psychologist with twenty five years of experience helping people with their relationships, marriages, and divorces. Dr. Gabardi maintains a private practice in Beaverton, Oregon providing psychotherapy, mediation, and divorce consultation. She is also author of The *Quick Guide to Co-Parenting After Divorce: Three Steps to Your Children's Healthy Adjustment*. **www.gabardi.com**

Benjamin D. Garber, Ph.D., is a psychologist practicing in New Hampshire. He works around the world in family law to helps parents, courts, schools and institutions better understand and serve the needs of children and families in transition. Dr. Garber's latest book, *Holding Tight, Letting Go* will be available in the fall of 2015. **www.HealthyParent.com**

Angela C. Gleason has been preparing to write children's books on blended families for many years—and now she's published her books under Blended Books. She has had several years of hands on experience being a step mother. As a child she had a stepfather for all of her teen years. She has always had a dream of sharing her experiences with others in order to help them get through difficult situations while going through a divorce and becoming part of a blended family. What better way to do this than to write children's books about divorce and different blended family situations. **www.blendedbooks.com**

Renee Harrison & **Jeremy Kossen** are transformers. They continue to build their passionate DivorceBuddy tribe through our DivorceBuddy podcast show, with the goal of transforming how people divorce. Their focus is to change divorcing couples' mindsets and encourage them to always put kids first, work collaboratively—not against one another—and at all costs, to *stay out of court*. Their ultimate goal is to build a membership platform that will host various online courses created by ethical divorce professionals, educating divorcing couples on the concepts outlined above. They strongly believe divorce should first be approached through a therapeutic and transformative family focus. **www.divorcebuddy.com**

Norman Hartnell is a family solicitor, mediator, collaborative lawyer and arbitrator with one of the UKs largest specialist family law practices. **www.thefamilylawco.com**

Jamie Kautz, MSW, LICSW has worked with children and families for over 22 years. She currently works as a mental health consultant to community mental health and foster care agencies in Washington State.

Dan Keusal, M.S., LMFT, is a Jungian Psychotherapist, astrologer, writer, and workshop leader based in Seattle. His acclaimed e-newsletter, *Living with Purpose and Passion*, and more information about his work, can be found at **www.dankeusal.com.**

Houston Kraft is a Keynote Speaker, Leadership Trainer, and Kindness Advocate who specializes in working with middle school through college-age students. **www.houstonkraft.com**

Dr. Nicole Letourneau holds the Palix/Alberta Children's Hospital Foundation Research Chair in Parent-Infant Mental Health and is Research Coordinator of RESOLVE Alberta. Her CHILD (Child Health Intervention and Longitudinal Development) Studies Program develops and tests interventions that support the development of infants and children growing up in families affected by toxic stressors, including parental depression, addictions, intimate partner violence and low-income. Her book *Scientific Parenting: What Science Reveals about Parental Influence*, published by Dundurn in 2013, describes much of this research. Learn more at **www.childstudies.ca**

Kristin Little, MA, MS, LMHC is a Licensed Mental Health Counselor providing individual counseling for adults and adolescents as well as family therapy; she also serves as a Collaborative Child Specialist for families during and post-divorce. **www.kristinlittlecounseling.com**

Anne Lucas, MA, LMHC is a therapist, coach, teacher / trainer and mediator. She works as a divorce coach in Collaborative Practice and has a mediation practice specializing in parenting plans and parent conflict. She is the owner and Clinical Director of The Evergreen Clinic in Kirkland, a multi-disciplinary mental health clinic where she works with couples in all stages of transition. **www.theevergreenclinic.com**

Suzy Miller is the creator of Divorce in a Box and author of *Your Alternative Divorce Guide*. To stay out of divorce court, check out Suzy's website. **www.startingovershow.com**

Christopher Mills is a psychotherapist, mediator, family consultant and author. He is passionate about interdisciplinary practice, especially in support of healthy divorce processes, and is the first practitioner in the UK to offer individual therapy-based supervision to family lawyers of the type that is mandatory for other mental health and social welfare professionals. **www.chrismills.uk.com**

Deborah Moskovitch is a Divorce Coach supporting people to have more positive outcomes from their divorce, for a happier and healthier future. Responding to the demand for "neutral" support, Deborah founded The Smart Divorce® to provide divorce information, support, divorce coaching and powerful educational tools to empower and free people during this difficult time. As a leading Divorce Coach worldwide, she provides unique divorce support services. Deborah is the best-selling author of *The Smart Divorce, The Smart Divorce Smart Guides*, and The Smart Divorce Audios. **www.thesmartdivorce.com**

Patricia Ann Russell is the author of *The Divorce Ceremony: Healing Spiritually and Divorcing Amicably in Twelve Weeks*, as well as President, The Divorce Foundation and The Russell Consulting Group. **www.trcgconsulting.com**

Wendi Schuller is a nurse, NLP, and hypnotherapist who helps school children and their parents adjust to divorce. She is a contributor to *The Divorce Magazine* and other publications. Her second book, *The Global Guide to Divorce* is being published in London, October, 2015. **www.globalguidetodivorce.com**

Kevin R. Scudder is a Collaborative attorney and mediator based in Seattle, Washington. Kevin embraced a collaborative, peacemaking approach to resolving conflict in 2008, and since then has been an active and well-regarded blogger, trainer and ambassador of Collaborative Practice. **www.scudderlaw.net**

Matt Sossi is an attorney and Executive Director of "Kids First Parents Second." For a complete published copy of the *I'm Just a Kid* manual, contact **mattsossi@bsossi.com**. **www.kidsfirstparentssecond.com**

Debra Synovec founder of Whole Mediation and Consulting Services, P.C. provides skillful mediation services in Seattle, Washington. Debra has been helping families solve and prevent conflict for over 25 years. She specializes in face-to-face, early stage mediation including divorce, domestic partnership dissolution, and estate planning. She is known for her ability to integrate legal, financial and relationship issues by combining her unique background acquired as an attorney, CPA, CDFA and social worker. Debra has achieved Advanced Practitioner Mediator status of the Academy of Professional Family Mediators. She holds a J.D. from William Mitchell College of Law, a B.S. in Accounting from the University of Minnesota, and a B.A. in Social Work from St. Cloud State College. **www.wholemediation.com**

Muriel Walls is an attorney specializing in family law in Ireland for more than thirty years. In addition to leading many ground-breaking cases, she has written and lectured extensively on the social impact of the changing nature of family law issues within her country. She is an accredited mediator and is active in many national and international family law and campaigning organizations. She can be reached at **www.wallsandtoomey.ie.**

ACKNOWLEDGEMENTS

Felicia & Karen

A project like this involves so many helpful and supportive people that to attempt to name them all risks accidentally leaving someone out. First and foremost, our thanks is extended to all of our clients throughout the years who have shown grace and dignity in the face of heart-wrenching decisions as their intimate partnerships and family structures transition to their next chapters. Allowing us to hold the space for their deepest fears, strongest emotions, and best hopes for themselves and their children has been a privilege from which we have learned so much. They have helped us help others.

We want to thank every pioneer we've been so lucky to work with as part of the Collaborative Practice community—that list is long and we are full of deep appreciation. The facilitative mediators who came long before us have spearheaded *divorce without court* and family-centered resolutions for restructuring families —you have been our teachers.

And we want to thank Tim Jones and the Covestream Team, Shane Kantzer and Charles "Chuck" Tuck. Without their talent, expertise, good humor and guidance, this video book would still be *just an idea*. Leigh Noffsinger, JD, jumped in with her amazing editing skills to bring clarity and valuable feedback to sharpen the content—thank you Leigh. Debra Synovec of Whole Mediation gave us that great video clip of her in action—thank you, Debra! As with *The Co-Parents' Handbook*, design inside and out creates a look and feel that truly represents the material—a big, huge shout-out to Kathryn Campbell for her artistic and stylistic talent—you did it again!

Felicia

Of course, I have to extend my utmost, heartfelt gratitude to Karen Bonnell, my dear friend, colleague, and co-conspirator in all things that challenge the limitations of our intermingled professions. Thank you, Karen, for inviting me to share in this next project of yours to such an extent after the success of your book, *The Co-Parents' Handbook*. Following Karen in her passion to encourage families to focus on those who often can't speak for themselves when their family is changing - the children - has inspired me immensely, adding a special element to my own work with clients.

I also owe much gratitude to Jamie Kautz, Margy Clair, and Muriel Walls, professional colleagues who, through our work together and shared philosophies that families don't belong in courtrooms, have become the dearest of friends. Each has contributed to this project in their special way, some generously sharing intimate, personal insights from their own lives, experiences which undoubtedly influence their professional work and add so much depth to this project.

Personally, my wholehearted love and gratitude goes to my wonderful husband, Tom Gross, for his never-ending patience and encouragement with my work overall, but especially during the intensive months of working on this project. His excitement for this project never wavered. Thank you for always being my rock when I need it most (and for keeping me fed!)

Finally, (although realistically first and foremost), I could not have worked on this project, nor do the other work I do, without the foundation provided to me by my own parents, John and Patricia Kumler. They somehow figured out how to raise four, strong daughters during the tumultuous 1960's and 70's in the healthiest child-centered way: boundless love and encouragement, yet with firm boundaries and grounding. Thanks, Mom and Dad! You have my eternal love and gratitude.

Karen

Felicia and I met when she was already a leader in the fields of mediation and Collaborative Practice, and I was just beginning to emerge from years as a psychotherapist into the realm of Collaborative divorce and co-parent coaching. She has been an important part of my brain trust, my mentor, my cheerleader...and dear friend. She's the one who taught me to say, "How hard can it be?" Fearless, she is.

You have met many of my colleagues as contributors to this book—to each and every contributor, near and far, I'm very grateful for your willingness to join as a "chorus of voices" to inspire parents everywhere to choose the best separation / divorce path possible for themselves and their children.

And lastly, I will always want to acknowledge my two adult children, Ben Werth and Ali Sameti, and my son-in-law, Ardie Sameti for their good humor and inspiration. As children of divorce, they continue to pursue the meaning and value of commitment, love, relationship and family-in-all-its-forms and share with me their under-standings of life—for this I'm eternally grateful.

AUTHOR BIOGRAPHIES

Karen Bonnell, ARNP, MS is a board-certified clinical nurse specialist with over 30 years of experience working with individuals, couples, and teams. As a divorce and co-parent coach, Karen has dedicated her work to resolving conflicts thoughtfully—one person, one couple or one family at a time.

A native Detroiter, Karen moved to the Seattle area in 1981 after completing her education at The University of Michigan, Ann Arbor. She has served on the faculties of Schoolcraft College, Eastern Michigan University, University of Michigan, and Seattle-Pacific University—where she taught psychiatric nursing. After teaching and years of clinical practice, she has recently included writing as part of her professional endeavors. She wrote and published *The Co-Parents' Handbook* in July 2014. She is the author of "Co-Parent Coaching: The Next Page in the Collaborative Playbook," featured in *The Collaborative Review*: The International Academy of Collaborative Professionals, Fall 2015 / Volume 15, Issue 2.

Karen has served on the board of King County Collaborative Law and was a founding member of the Collaborative Professionals of Washington. She is a member of the International Academy of Collaborative Professionals and Academy of Professional Family Mediators. She regularly presents on topics related to divorce and co-parent coaching, as well as advanced communication skills.

Karen lives in the foothills of the Cascade Range outside Seattle. She values the lessons learned in the "school of hard knocks" in her experience of creating a two-home family before divorce coaching existed. Her two adult children are her daily inspiration for the beauty of love, forgiveness, and trust in the capacity of family in all its forms. In her free time, you'll find her exploring national parks and hiking trails with her aim-and-shoot camera.

Felicia Malsby Soleil, JD is the principal of Family Law Resolutions, PS, a family law firm located in Gig Harbor, Washington. Her focus is collaborative divorce and legal separation, mediation, and consulting on all matters associated with transitioning couples and families. She was named the 2010 Family Law Attorney of the Year by the Family Law Section of the Tacoma-Pierce County Bar Association, recognizing her leadership in establishing Collaborative Law locally, as well as throughout Washington State. She is a founder and past president of Collaborative Professionals of Washington

An Ohio native, she graduated from Guilford College in Greensboro, North Carolina, with a Bachelor of Science in Sociology, and then earned her law degree from the University of Puget Sound School of Law (now Seattle University School of Law) in 1992. She has been a resident of Gig Harbor, Washington for more than 25 years, after locating to Washington as a military spouse. Felicia practiced traditional family law litigation for more than a decade before evolving her practice to one focused primarily on dispute resolution advocacy.

After completing extensive training in collaborative law, mediation, collaborative team building, and coaching, she has developed and presented multiple educational workshops and trainings for fellow legal professionals. Now, with *The Parenting Plan Handbook*, Felicia is expanding her passion to deliver valuable resources and education directly to families and those who work to support them.

To help maintain balance in her life, Felicia enjoys quiet days working in her gardens, golfing with friends, and visiting new places with her husband, Tom.

AUTHOR CONTACT INFORMATION

For more information about Karen Bonnell's work, please visit the following:

www.theparentingplanhandbook.com

www.coachmediateconsult.com

Facebook.com/karenbonnellcmc

Twitter.com/Karenbonnellcmc

To reach Karen, you can contact her through the following:

Karen@coachmediateconsult.com

For more information about Felicia Malsby Soleil, please visit:

www.familylawresolutions.com

www.coachingwithfelicia.com

You can reach Felicia through the following:

Felicia@familylawresolutions.com

felicia@coachingwithfelicia.com

THE CO-PARENTS' HANDBOOK

Raising Well-Adjusted, Resilient and Resourceful Kids in a Two-Home Family from Little Ones to Young Adults

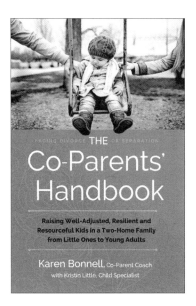

Karen Bonnell with Kristin Little

With a tested "here's how" approach, **The Co-Parents' Handbook** helps parents confidently take on the challenges of raising children in two homes. Addressing parents' questions about the emotional impact of separation, conflict, grief and recovery, the authors skillfully provide a roadmap for all members of the family to safely navigate through separation / divorce and beyond. Parents discover through practical guidance how to move from angry / hurt partners to constructive, successful co-parents. The pages are chock-full of helpful strategies to resolve day-to-day issues in an easy-to-use format. This book is here to answer questions, help parents **co-parent** and ensure kids **thrive**!

"Karen Bonnell's handbook is very comprehensive, detailed and engaging, with story examples and tips on almost every page. There are many books out now about co-parenting in divorce, but this is the most comprehensive I have seen for parents whose children are their highest priority."

—**Bill Eddy**, LCSW, Esq, President of the High Conflict Institute, and creator of the *New Ways for Families.*

"This book contains the absolute essence of practical, healthy co-parenting for two homes. Sound guidance, clear protocols, and compassionate insights—a much needed resource! A 'must read' not only for co-parents, but also for anyone interested in how to support changing families."

—**Anne Lucas**, MA, LMHC, Psychotherapist, Mediator, Divorce Coach and adjunct faculty at Saybrook University, President of Collaborative Professionals of Wasington.